TURNING POINTS
IN
WOMEN'S LIVES

Volume Two

Los Ranchos, NM

Turning Points In Women's Lives

Volume Two

Shirley L. Patterson and Susan A. Cho, Editors

Nuevo Books
Los Ranchos, New Mexico
2015

© 2015, Nuevo Books

All rights reserved.
Nuevo Books
Los Ranchos, New Mexico
www.NuevoBooks.com

Printed in the U.S.A.

Book design by Paul Rhetts
Cover photograph by Shirley Patterson

Library of Congress Cataloging-in-Publication Data

Turning points in women's lives : Volume Two /
Shirley L. Patterson and Susan A. Cho, editors.
p. cm.
ISBN 978-1-936745-12-8 (pbk. : alk. paper)
1. Older women--United States--Biography.
2. Women--United States--Biography.
3. Women--United States--Social conditions--20th century.
4. Women--United States--Social conditions--21st century.
5. Life change events--United States--Case studies.
6. Influence (Psychology)--Case studies.
7. United States--Biography.
8. Retired women--New Mexico--Albuquerque--Biography.
9. Albuquerque (N.M.)--Biography.
I. Patterson, Shirley L., 1933-
II. Cho, Susan A., 1943-
HQ1064.U5T88 2012
920.720973--dc23
2011053254

Cover: Fourth of July Canyon, New Mexico by Shirley Patterson

DEDICATED TO

each committed, wise and thoughtful woman at La Vida Llena who opened a window into her life in the story she wrote for this book;
AND
Marcia Hunsberger, whose gentle caring and wisdom inspired all her family and friends, and whose life ended far too soon. (For this book her husband, Gerald, has shared an episode in Marcia's life that depicts how her love of teaching shaped her commitment to others.)

CONTENTS

ACKNOWLEDGEMENTS

Our thanks...to Judy Munsterman for typing stories for women who were unable to type their own...to those families and friends who encouraged and assisted the writing of stories...to Patrick who rescued us when computer problems threatened our progress...to Linda Givens, Executive Director of La Vida Llena, for her support of this project and for committing La Vida Llena resources to provide a book signing event to launch this book...to Barbe Awalt and Paul Rhetts of Nuevo Books for their helpful suggestions and publishing expertise...to our friends who encouraged us to do this second book.

The Editors

FOREWORD

When I wrote the Foreword to the first volume of *Turning Points in Women's Lives*, I knew it was an important book. Not only for the talented and varied writers, but for anyone fortunate enough to read what they wrote. It is no less so for Volume Two.

A continuation of the important compendium of experiences, feelings, ups, downs, successes and accomplishments of the women of La Vida Llena, this book further enlightens and fascinates us as to the varied lives these women have lived and continue to live. Just as no two women are alike, no two stories are alike, and therein lies their value.

I am reminded of one of the tenets from the mindfulness movement: paying attention to thoughts and feelings without judging them — without believing, that there's a "right" or "wrong" way to think or feel in a given moment. The writers have expanded on that to encompass how they thought, felt, and acted in a given period of, or experience in, their well-seasoned lives.

Like the first volume, this book gives a glimpse of lives well lived, and the events and people that helped to shape them.

Take a journey through the 20th century – and parts of the 21st – with these women. You will be enriched for your travels.

Martha Burk, Ph.D.

Martha Burk is a women's rights advocate who is former Chair of the National Council of Women's Organizations. She is currently Money Editor for *Ms.* magazine, and has a syndicated column and radio show, "Equal Time with Martha Burk," originating at KSFR Public Radio in Santa Fe, N.M. She served as Senior Advisor for Women's Issues to Governor Bill Richardson of New Mexico, and is the author of *Your Voice, Your Vote: The Savvy Woman's Guide to Power, Politics, and the Change We Need.* Her motto, "If I can't dance, I won't come to your revolution," comes from the early 20th century labor activist, Emma Goldman. She resides in Corrales, New Mexico, with her husband, Ralph Estes.

INTRODUCTION

Turning Points in Women's Lives, Volume Two is a continuing exploration of significant influences in the lives of women in their 70s, 80s and 90s. These women live at La Vida Llena (LVL), a Life-Care continuing care retirement community established in Albuquerque, New Mexico, in 1983.

The original book, *Turning Points in Women's Lives, From the 20th to the 21st Century* (2012), evolved from a grassroots organization, The Gathering of Women, at La Vida Llena. The editors of these books were instrumental in starting and developing The Gathering of Women. It has met for 10 months each year since August 2008. The programs focus on how each woman presenter, be she a resident or from the larger Albuquerque community, "moved from here to there" in her life.

The women who attended The Gathering were enthused by the personal stories. Over time, the group experience led to a sense of kinship, empowerment and trust among the women. In addition, the editors, drawing from their professional social work backgrounds, knew the value of the mental health concepts of reminiscence and life review. The process of looking back and reviewing a life situation can provide an opportunity to put that experience into a more balanced view of self.

Taking into account these factors, the editors decided to invite women who attended The Gathering to write stories to be published in a book. To encourage a thoughtful life review and to bring focus to the book, the editors developed a single question to which each author should respond — **"What person, event or group significantly influenced your life? How?"**

The success of this first book created interest in doing a second volume. Families and friends of the story authors were excited to find their familiar stories in print. Each author's satisfaction in the process of thinking through her story and discovering its impact on her life inspired the editors. The community at large seemed intrigued by the idea of ordinary women, who have lived through the enormous cultural and historical changes of the 20th century and beyond, having the opportunity to share a significant part of their life journeys. All were heartened when *Turning Points …* was a winner in the Anthology category of the New Mexico-Arizona Book Awards and also won a first place in Editing from the New Mexico Press Women.

For *Volume Two*, women residents of LVL were asked to address the same question as in the first book. Each would write about the influence of a person, group or event that played a significant role in her life and how it gave direction to who she became.

The stories in *Volume Two* replicate the original book in their diversity. Two-thirds of the writers in each book were in their 80s and 90s. They are representative of the age of the residents who live at LVL. Their age is noteworthy for the interest and capability of these women to take on this task.

On the whole, the women of LVL are well educated and represent careers in teaching, psychology, social work, medicine, nursing, and business. Others chose to fulfill their lives through raising a family and often did significant volunteer work. Many of the authors did it all.

These women were attending college in the 1940s and 1950s, long before the impact of the second wave of the women's movement (in the 1960s and 1970s) when more doors were beginning to open for women. Perhaps more importantly, they were in grade school when girls were shown few options for advanced achievement. They were often counseled to become a secretary, a teacher, or perhaps, a nurse.

There is great geographic diversity among the authors. A large majority, of course, are from the United States, mostly from the West, Midwest and East with fewer from the South. Four were born abroad to American parents, and three were born in Europe to European parents. Their differing origins make for uniqueness in their stories.

Among the significant influences written about, many are a family member or other person with the story reflecting a historical context, such as WWII, the social upheaval of the 60s and 70s, the sexual revolution, or the electronic age. The significant influence in other stories is a historical or health event, such as feeling the impact of the testing of the atomic bomb or having a Down syndrome child, that affected individual and family development.

In sum, these stories reflect how women share history and an immediate understanding of how it has been to travel common paths and experiences that encompass love, shame, joy, sadness, self-doubt and self-confidence. Yet, each story is a unique tale of how its author survived, persevered and came to terms with her one life in her own way.

Shirley L. Patterson and Susan A. Cho, Editors

A Promise Kept
by
Dorothy M. Barbo

On a frosty cold Wisconsin winter night, my brother and I arrived home from an evening of sleigh-riding with the church youth group. My father who had advanced colon cancer was already asleep. He had not talked much during the day. Mother called us at 2 a.m. to say our father was having difficulty breathing. We were with him when he died within a short time. Our family doctor came quickly and pronounced my father's death. Then he hurried out the door and left my mother standing with two teenagers, ages 15 and 13, wondering what to do next.

Mother was very distressed and needed someone to talk with and help. I did the best I could until morning when family members came. I made a promise that night that when I became a doctor I would take time with families to help them through those difficult moments.

At age 10, I had made a firm decision to become a physician after seeing a bad road accident when no one seemed to know what to do and how to help. I concluded that one needed to be trained as a doctor to be able to help appropriately.

1

As years passed, I continued my education — taking all the science and math available. My goal did not change. At Asbury University in Kentucky, I majored in biology and took all the pre-med prerequisites. My major professor, Dr. C.B. Hamann, encouraged me as I applied for medical school. My first choice was the University of Wisconsin as it was in my home state. Marquette University in Milwaukee turned down my application. In the spring since I had not heard from Wisconsin, Dr. Hamann arranged an interview for me at Vanderbilt University, Nashville, Tenn. I was placed on the alternate list there. Finally in mid-April I received a letter of acceptance from the University of Wisconsin School of Medicine. I began my studies in Madison in September 1954 as one of the nine women in a class of 80. I was on my way to achieving my goal.

During my first year of medical school my brother, who was completing his degree in chemical engineering, was working at McArdle Cancer Labs at the University of Wisconsin. He introduced me to the researchers who were developing new cancer drugs. One of the early new drugs they were researching was fluorouracil (5-FU). It was in clinical use before I graduated. This research sparked my interest in oncology.

My training continued in Milwaukee with post-graduate work in Obstetrics and Gynecology. Following that was a fellowship in gynecological oncology at Marquette University School of Medicine. During those days, the famous Pap test for cervical cancer screening was making a big impact on finding cervical cancers early when there was a better chance for cure. Commonly many women died in the hospital with advanced cancers. As I cared for them, I had the opportunity to fulfill my teenage promise to listen and share with families the status of their loved ones. It takes extra time and energy to care – but that is what makes all the difference for me.

In 1968, I joined the Board of Global Missions of the United Methodist Church and went to teach and train at the Ludhiana

Christian Medical College in the state of Punjab in northwest India. There the need for care of women with gynecological cancers was great. During those years, Brown Hospital had the only radiation therapy treatment for cancers in Punjab. It was a very busy time of clinical work, operating and teaching in the medical school. The majority of the women's cancers were cervical, and women came great distances for treatment. Sadly, many had very advanced stages of disease. The women and their families came to learn the diagnosis and hear the truth about treatments. They wanted to know if they could be helped. Usually, I had to communicate through nurse or physician interpreters. I discovered that time and honesty were crucial in imparting hope when it was good news and compassion when it was bad news. Such conversations take emotional energy and strength.

Adding up the numbers of patients treated I discovered I cared for about 400 gynecological cancer cases in each of the four years I lived and worked in Ludhiana. In addition, I treated many benign diseases, surgical cases, normal deliveries, and complicated obstetrical conditions. Life was never boring, though many times it was overwhelming with yet another emergency.

In 1972, I completed my term with the Board of Global Missions and returned to the United States. I took a teaching position at the Medical College of Pennsylvania in Philadelphia (originally the Women's Medical College). There, in addition to having a large clinical practice, I was very involved with teaching medical students and resident physicians.

Cancer care was a prominent part of my work for most of those next years. I was involved with a course for first-year medical students to introduce them to cancer — the types, treatments, statistics and outcomes. Many students came with the idea that all cancers were hopeless, and most people died. We were attempting to teach them that there was hope as many cancers were treatable, especially when found early. In one of the sessions, we asked patients to come and share their cancer stories. A patient of mine, a lovely woman who taught art in the public schools, graciously agreed to come and talk about her treatment for cervical cancer. She described how her treatment was successful and that she had an active life. I was surprised when she shared that, when I gave her the "bad news" that she had cancer, the most important thing I had told her was that there was HOPE she could be cured and we should go for it! It would be a team effort, and she would be an important part of the team. Hearing her talk to the class, I realized I had again fulfilled my promise of many years ago.

One woman who was referred to me had an advanced rare, aggressive cervical cancer with heavy and continuous bleeding. Though the treatment stopped the hemorrhages, the cancer progressed. She was hospitalized when her family could no longer care for her at home. One night she took a turn for the worse and called her family to come. Only the daughter, who lived some distance away, came. She arrived before her mother died.

When spending time with the daughter, I discovered she had no idea what to do next, whom to call, or what arrangements needed to be made. It was now 2 a.m. I could not send her away alone to drive through a very dangerous area of the city. Along with the help of caring nurses, we found a bed so she could rest until morning. We wrote down several things that needed to be done including talking with her priest about arrangements. She has always remained grateful. Again I fulfilled my promise.

Only later in my mature years did I realize that our beloved family doctor, C.A. Olsen, M.D., had hurried out the door on that cold January night in 1947 because he too was distressed at my father's death. They were good friends. He was always wonderful to care for my mother over the years. He wrote a letter of recommendation for me for medical school. He helped me get work in the summer to earn for college and medical school. He did care!

After 20 years in Philadelphia, it was time to move on. I was recruited to the University of New Mexico (UNM) School of Medicine in Albuquerque in 1991. Though hoping to have a less stressful practice at UNM, I again was needed to work in gynecological oncology and the NM Department of Health Breast and Cervical Cancer Early Detection Program. A new culture of language and understanding of the Native Americans was an interesting and rewarding challenge.

In 1999, I retired from UNM to focus on teaching, training, and traveling internationally for medical missions. So life continues with opportunities to listen, learn, and care for those who are hurting or ill and to do it all with compassion, love and hope.

April 16, 1954, Bruce
by
Lori Castle

On April 16, 1954, I had been in the hospital in Los Alamos, New Mexico, for two days trying to postpone premature delivery of my second child, who would join my husband, Ed, our daughter, Betsy, age 2, and me. However, in the late afternoon, Bruce Alan Voorhees entered the world, weighing 4 pounds, 6 ounces. A turning point in my life had been reached.

As I groggily became aware of all around me, I realized Ed was upset, and the nurses were very solicitous. I assumed this was because the baby was so tiny that he would have to stay in the hospital for a while. Before I was discharged, my obstetrician, our pediatrician and Ed entered my room to give me the news that our son had Mongolism and would likely be severely mentally retarded. The pediatrician said, "You should not take this child home from the hospital. You should not learn to love him." We assumed the doctor knew the right thing to do.

Within a few days, we learned the New Mexico residential facility for persons with mental retardation (MR) had no vacancy and a long waiting list. One private facility existed, but its cost was beyond our means. Ed and I began a long-term search for information about MR in general and Mongolism in particular. We learned that such children placed in institutions at birth often died by the age of 2, mainly due to lack of being moved leading to non-development of the brain.

We took Bruce home when he was 10 days old, and we naturally learned to love him. He was a quiet child, content with life. We slowly came to an acceptance of his limitations. My life as a homemaker revolved around our family of four. Less than a year later we were joined by another son, Ron. Life went on at a frenzied pace for some time — we moved to a larger home and Betsy and Bruce came down with measles.

When our life began to settle into something of a routine, a Los Alamos couple advertised that they were seeking other parents of children with mental handicaps to form a group for mutual support. We called the number given and joined two other sets of parents. We set out together to find what we could do to help our children.

Ed and I did not fully realize it then, but we had begun 20 years of intensive effort in getting services for our child and others like him. We attended our other two children's events through the years — church, scouting, school, and sports events. We assumed some leadership, though we concentrated on the needs of children with MR.

Public services available to persons with MR in all of New Mexico were: the one state institution in Los Lunas and one public school Special Education class in Albuquerque. The latter was only for children with tested IQs over 50, which our son was not likely to have. Soon both a National and a New Mexico Association for Retarded Children (N.M.A.R.C. to us) were founded, and the Kennedy family developed public awareness of the needs of Rosemary Kennedy and other persons with MR.

In 1954 we had been told that Mongolism resulted from high fever, often from measles, in the mother during the first six to eight weeks of pregnancy. When Bruce was about 5, research in Europe found that human cells have 23 pairs of chromosomes, not 24 as previously believed. They further discovered that Mongolism was a syndrome in which one of the smaller pairs divided improperly, with part of the chromosome attaching itself to a different pair. The condition was renamed Down syndrome for the researcher who described the condition in the 1860s. So much for "measles" in weeks six to eight! We also learned that about 50% of persons with Down syndrome are born with the same kind of heart defect from which lung damage can result. Bruce had this "cushion defect."

Later, when Bruce was 7, our local school board had agreed to set up its first Special Education class. They hired a teacher and started a class that included Bruce. The teacher did not want children of Bruce's level (there were three), saying they were not the responsibility of the public schools. She got them removed by Thanksgiving. At parents' urging, an aide was hired for the class and in late winter the three were readmitted. The teacher still didn't like having them and resigned at the end of the year. But the class continued and until age 21 Bruce was in school where he made progress and made friends.

We needed statewide action and support for education for all children in N.M. To that end, we attended the N.M. Legislature for many years. During one of the first sessions we attended, a rancher/legislator drawled, "Well, I know what we do on our ranch with defective horses." We shuddered but kept seeking services.

I was spending about 30 hours each week meeting with parents, working with our special children locally and seeking the support of local and state agencies, as did other parents. Gradually Special Ed classes came into being across the state. The N.M. Association for Retarded Citizens (new name — Children changed to Citizens), received a Kennedy Foundation grant for a state-wide residential camp. At age 8, Bruce attended. He insisted on taking his teddy bear, Lala. The counselors reported Bruce just observed — until a dance closed the week's activities. Accompanied by Lala, Bruce happily danced and smiled.

We started a local day camp in Los Alamos, which I helped or-
ganize and lead the first two years. Then we mothers decided that,
with a dozen campers, it was time to hire a director. We raised funds
town-wide and were able to hire a talented director. We also began
a Saturday morning recreation program at a church. A wonderful
woman volunteered her time as leader, assisted by parents and high
school volunteers. Many of the young volunteers went into helping
professions, including our Betsy and Ron.

Special Olympics games, sponsored by the Kennedy Foundation, started. Jaycees helped us parents in training and in running
local and area meets. Some of us took the participants to state Special Olympics meets, stayed with them in the dorms, and helped
with all the details, including cheering on our group and settling
pre-event "butterflies." Bruce's big event was swimming.

When our special children grew older, a high school class was
opened. Though his diploma did not mean the same as for "normal" youth, the highlight of Bruce's life was going through graduation just like he had seen his siblings do in earlier years.

We were able to start a local sheltered workshop, and we realized we needed a group home. I was to serve on the planning committee. Then my marriage of 27 years foundered. I resigned from
the committee, as I needed a full-time job and schooling to train for
further employment. The other children had gotten much of their
education and were no longer at home full-time. Bruce went into a
new privately-run group home in northern New Mexico, where he
adjusted well. His needs had dominated my preceding 21 years, and
now my life needed to turn elsewhere.

I trained as a computer operator and then as a programmer. In
1978, I moved to Albuquerque to work for EG&G, a tech company,
on contract to Sandia Lab. Though I was farther from Bruce, we
were together regularly. Later I was able to get Bruce into the excellent group home program run by the Albuquerque Association for
Retarded Citizens, now known as ARCA.

After several years in Albuquerque, I helped start a mature singles group at my downtown church. One of our activities was a monthly brunch after church. Bruce liked to attend church and the brunches with me. At one Sunday brunch, to Bruce's delight, the Watermelon Mountain Jug Band played. He sat as close to the band as possible. A fairly new member of our singles group felt sorry that Bruce had to sit alone; so he moved up to sit with Bruce. Once again, Bruce provided a turning point to my life, as that man was Jack Castle. Bruce joined his two siblings in being my attendants when Jack and I were married in 1982.

By 1987, Bruce's health was so poor that he could no longer be at the group home, and he moved home with Jack and me. No step-father could have been more accepting and loving than was Jack. When Bruce's heart finally gave out in early 1992, he was 37. Betsy and her younger son from Los Alamos had visited him in the after-noon. Around 6 p.m. Ron, his wife, Jack and I were there as Bruce took his final breath.

Bruce's life had changed our lives, especially mine — and as-suredly for the better. I realized all those with handicaps are PER-SONS first, with the hopes and emotions of all people. I developed self-confidence through seeking governmental and agency help and through working directly with persons with handicaps. Most of all, Bruce's unconditional love for others helped me follow his example.

The Shy Girl
by
Phyllis Davis

I was a very shy child and young adult. In my first two foster homes, this was no problem. In my third and last one it was such a disaster that I was considered to be sub-par in intelligence and was so treated. So how did I become a stewardess with American Airlines? How did I even get through the interview? I lied. I lied about my height. The airline limit was 5 feet 6 inches, and I was 5 feet 7 inches. I persisted, and they hired me.

Now I was away from "home," and that was a big help. I attended flight school and finally had the guidance I needed. Since nobody at the airline knew I was "deficient," they gave me several jobs to do and expected me to do them. Jobs? I thought I was a stewardess! Yes and no. Management started showing me letters they had received from both civilians and high American Airlines corporate officers who were praising my work. It seems I was good!

Then came a "gig" representing American Airlines at the opening of a theater in Hollywood. Yes, I was stationed in Los Angeles with 200 other stewardesses.

Next, I was assigned to go to the Douglas Aircraft plant to critique a new plane being developing for American Airlines that had decided it wanted to start overnight sleeper service from Los Angeles to New York City. Really! I was met at Douglas by six designers and engineers to evaluate the cabin mock-up. Six men, all over 6 feet tall, were very eager and proud to present their new concoction. I took one look at the cabin arrangement and my heart sank. Douglas designers and engineers had gone to the Pullman Company and acquired Pullman sleepers that were only slightly smaller than the standard Pullman berths. They (the six-footers) showed me (the five-plus-footer) how the beds worked. The five-plus-footer knew how they worked, having spent much of my youth in Pullman berths. Guess what — I could not reach the hole for the T-shaped key that opened the bed. Six smiling faces dropped simultaneously while one kept smiling. Mine. My report on the mock-up was, "It doesn't work." The whole idea, plane and all, was scrapped!

The next big moment came at my exit interview. I was leaving so I could marry. (In those days a married woman could not work for the airlines.) They told me they were sorry to see me leave as they had selected me to be the Chief Stewardess for Los Angeles Station! I should have stayed as the marriage did not work out. I could have gone back, but I am a firm believer in "You can't go home again."

The point of all this is that I was treated for the first time like a normal, intelligent person. Certain things were expected of me, I knew how to do them, and I prospered. I have never forgotten those lessons I learned. And my foster family saw I had suddenly turned into a normal human being. I had finally learned how to deal with them.

From my airline experience, I went on to bigger and better jobs — I was a civilian working for the Army as a logistical staff officer editing logistical reports and as Report Control Officer for the division.

Upon arriving in Albuquerque with my second husband (Army

retired), I dove into Archaeology. Most people here at La Vida Llena consider Archaeology as my career. It was only my third! And it all started with being an airline stewardess where I learned to value myself and have confidence in my abilities.

From a Sheltered Life to the Working World
by
Sue DuBroff

I was born in Cincinnati and have one sister. Our family was fairly well off, so I was sent to a private school and then college. I was expected to marry, have children, and do volunteer work. In looking back, I realize that I'd always wanted to go to work, but like many girls/women of my generation, I accepted what was expected. I married Warren DuBroff from Chicago, and my parents were not pleased that I was moving away. In any case they liked Warren and accepted our move to Chicago.

We had two sons, and after they were in school, I did volunteer work at the local hospital in the Medical Records Department. When I arrived for work, there was always a huge pile of records to go through and eventually code (diabetes was 250). I was good at this work, and I worked every bit as hard as the paid employees, even harder than some! All went well and then we got a new department head who was very snippy and much disliked. I no longer enjoyed the environment, but I discovered I liked the work.

I was beginning to understand that I had always "walked to a different drummer." Now, when I was a wife and mother, none of my friends worked, but I enjoyed it. I asked Warren if he would mind if I worked for money to see if I could, should the need arise, support myself. He was fine with this.

At the Medical Records Department, I was told I needed to work 20 hours a week in order to have a paid position. I figured out how to work the 20 hours a week and manage my home and family, as well. Because I didn't like our boss, I decided to see if I could become an Accredited Record Technician and work on my own. I took the training and passed the required exam to secure a federal license as an Accredited Record Technician.

In the Chicago area, a nursing home is required by Medicare to have someone with my qualifications check charting in medical records and give in-service training on how to meet Medicare standards for medical records. One of the physicians that I knew was Medical Director at a few nursing homes. When he heard I had a license, he gave me the name of some of his clients. I offered my services to them, and they hired me.

I established my company, Suzanne S. DuBroff & Assoc. My business grew, and I soon hired and trained two employees, Judy and Dot. I learned a lot about business and employees. I developed forms, established review processes, kept my employees trained, and made sure they were accurate in their work.

One day I got a call from one of my clients that Judy, one of my employees, was sick, and the JCAH (Joint Commission on Accreditation of Hospitals) was coming. They needed me to come and see that all was in order. I hustled over and to my dismay all of my forms marked Suzanne S. DuBroff & Assoc. now had Judy's name instead. When I came home and told Warren, he said, "Welcome to the real world." I was learning the up and down side of working for money and running a business.

I was able to work with the support I needed from my family. I learned that I was worth something. I, too, could be a breadwinner.

I Could Not Ask for More
by
Patricia Esterly

"We do not choose our family. It is a gift that God gives to us, as He gives them a gift, which is you." — Desmond Tutu

I can count many turning points in my 75 years. The first was at age 6 when my mother died, leaving nine children, ages 26 to 6. At the time of her death, the three eldest girls were married, and the oldest brother was in the Navy, but five of us were of school age and still living at home. Because our father traveled as a carpenter and was seldom in the house, we were left to conduct our lives as well as pos-  sible. There was little income, but pride in our heritage and faith in lessons from our mother's strict parenting guided us. Our grandparents were dead, but aunts and uncles were nearby and always encouraging.

My story begins at that point.

The remaining five of us were quickly removed from Catholic schools and enrolled in public school — Terrie, 16; Frances, 14; Clarence, 13; Jim, 10; and me, not yet 6. During my fourth, fifth and sixth grades we lived in a home with three large rooms that included the kitchen and no indoor plumbing. I remember that, being the youngest, I was last to leave for school after washing up and braiding my hair. I can just imagine that the part of the hair on the back of my head may have looked anything but straight!

Education was always my priority. As my grades were consistently at the top, and I won spelling competitions, my family was hopeful for my future, but another move often meant a different school or town. Occasionally, we had to depend on aunts and uncles for my day-to-day care as well.

From that time, I cannot count how many different schools I attended and households I lived in (some for a school year or two, some for only a summer). But families fed me and provided a safe environment, so I thrived. Unfortunately, college was out of the question in those days before lotteries and rich benefactors. I've learned that at one point a teacher spoke to my family about adopting me but my father, saying he didn't want to break up the family, refused her offer.

I married too young, not yet 17, but my new husband and I worked together to send him to college and when he had his first degree, we started a family. I was then 21 and working full time as a secretary in an upscale department store. I am now in a secure second marriage but am able to appreciate the lessons/experiences from the first as well.

It was always education that guided the raising of my children. I remember weighing any large expenses against the number of college classes the amount would cover. All four children attended good schools and now have advanced college degrees and children of their own. They are loving, independent, and emotionally mature in the raising of their children.

We humans bring with us lessons from good and bad experiences, so I can look back and be accepting of my somewhat chaotic life. My children remind me of the importance of simple acceptance.

I could not ask for more.

Journey to New Mexico and "My Mountains"
by
Janice T. Firkins

A toddler in the back seat of the car climbed up onto the rear shelf, looked out the window, and saw the sun shimmering on the road behind with "my mountains" around it. I was the little girl, and the sight was Tijeras Canyon. My father, diagnosed with tuberculosis, had gone to New Mexico to "chase" the cure. He had returned to Iowa, where my mother and I had been staying with my grandmother,  and was bringing us to be with him in the Albuquerque area.

At first we lived in the Sandia Mountains at Sedillo, N.M., for a year or so. We lived in a community of a large house with small guest houses around. The houses were occupied by others who were also "chasing" the cure until they were able to return to the work force of New Mexico. I was the only child in the group, and they all became my new family.

The men built huge kites — large enough to be seen in Albuquerque. The cable that flew the kites was very thick. It was very important that I stay away from it because I could be hurt. I had visions that I might get caught in the cable, and it would hoist me into the sky — never to be seen again. The kites kept us all entertained, but they also were to remind the city that we were still in the mountains fighting for health.

A clay croquet court was made and carefully rolled before the games. I was firmly told not to step on it before the game started. It was to be pristine. At late afternoon games, the cars would be parked in such an order that the lights could be turned on if the game lasted too long after the sun went down. Sometimes there were big concerns that the car batteries might run down before the game ended.

My father, an accountant, went to work for the Works Progress Administration (WPA). We moved to Santa Fe, N.M., a community of about 3,000 people. What a colorful, tradition-filled place. My memories are filled with wonder.

The annual Santa Fe Fiesta was a major event. I entered the Fiesta Pet Parade with my white Spitz dog, Fritzi. I wore my white sequined skirt with a white fiesta blouse. All the friends from Sedillo were there, helping with the costuming. As I was walking in the parade, I looked back and there was a flatbed truck with a big white bathtub containing a man taking a MUD bath. It was years before I realized the significance of this to water-starved Santa Feans. The burning of Zozobra, "Old Man Gloom," was a part of the Fiesta. He groaned and writhed with horrible anguish to take away the troubles and problems of all. A candlelight procession up the small hill ended the Fiesta. It is still in my mind's eye and perhaps ear. There was such a sense of quietude.

Later in the year we visited the little town of Madrid, N.M., where the miners had spent the whole year compiling all that was needed to create a Christmas scene. I remember that when we were close to the town and turned a curve in the road, the car lights were turned off. And, there was the STAR in the heavens. Then there were the shepherds with their herds and then the angels. We traveled on into town. We saw the family with the babe in the manger, shepherd boys with the lambs, angels, more animals and then the three wise men with camels and horses and MUSIC. There could have been herald trumpets, too.

My magical childhood turned into the realities of growing up. My father went to his WPA job and found his name on the list to be sent out into the work force of New Mexico. We moved to Albuquerque and Father went to work for an appliance store. I went to Monte Vista Elementary School. My sister was born.

One Sunday morning I was playing in the backyard when suddenly my father came out the back door saying we are going to the mountains to tell friends, who lived at Sandia Park, that the Japanese had bombed Pearl Harbor. Our friends did not have a telephone, and we needed to let them know that we were at WAR.

The war not only changed our life in New Mexico but also changed the world. My father became an air-raid warden for our neighborhood. He checked every night to make sure no one had any visible light leaking out of their homes. Mother folded bandages. There were no appliances to sell, so my father went to work for the Office of Price Administration, traveling throughout the state. I learned really fast that when going to the store it was more important to safeguard the rationing stamps in the book, than the money to pay the bill. Necessities were rationed: food, gas, shoes. As much as possible the nation's resources went into the war effort. We bought War Savings Stamps to go into books to purchase War Bonds.

Kirkland Air Force Base grew overnight. Airplanes constantly roared; soldiers were everywhere; pilots from all over the country, as well as a contingency from South America, were arriving. Thanks to our marvelous sun and weather, the planes could fly every day.

Life went on. But the poor man, Gordon, who worked for my dad repairing radios, suddenly disappeared. All his wife, Jay, knew about his whereabouts was a Post Office box number in Santa Fe. A close neighbor was up early one morning and saw a great blast of light south of town and felt the floor tremble. An event that changed everyone's life and the world had happened in New Mexico. The atomic bomb was being tested.

I was in the ninth grade and was assigned a class in physical science. I had had no previous science classes. I was totally out of my realm, particularly when I was expected to understand the operation of a combustion engine. The fellows loved it. However, the teacher of that class opened up my whole awareness of life. He introduced me to the power of energy that created "my mountains" and the universe.

My surrogate Uncle Gordon had been a classmate of Oppenheimer and was one of the mathematicians called into "the place that did not exist," Los Alamos. We all knew something was going on up there. That something, that explosion that shook the world, also shook Albuquerque and other communities in New Mexico. New people came in from all over the world bringing research and learning to lead New Mexico into space with ballistic missiles — just as 100 years ago a group of health seekers led us into new areas of health care with their research and learning.

Now my former students in southern New Mexico continue that research and learning and are taking us into space. While teaching I had begun to realize that I had been there before, there was more going on than just what some thought were flying saucers. Twenty-five years later, weird looking aircraft began landing at our little airport. I now see them in the news — drones. And we are off to space with civilian flights due to take off from the New Mexico's Spaceport America. A former student is on the Board of Directors. He has his doctorate from Stanford in space engineering. When he was in the Air Force, he was flying with his father one day when his father said, "You can tell me what you are doing?" He replied, "Dad, if I did, I'd have to shoot you."

I have come full circle. As a toddler I was uprooted to a new place and discovered "my mountains." I grew up and began to understand the power of energy, felt how it can be used and learned

how it impacts the world— including creating "my mountains."
Now, in this next phase of my journey at age 83, I smile as I drive
up the hill toward La Vida Llena and see the sun shimmering on
the road with "my mountains" beyond it.

These Accidental Events
by
Cecil B. Fish

Born in 1920 in Lebanon, Kentucky, I grew up in a family with a grandmother, parents and six brothers. After attending the public schools (segregated), I attended Mary Baldwin College, in Staunton, Virginia. I graduated with degrees in French and English and qualified to teach school. This was made possible by cramming in a bunch of education courses in my senior year to qualify to do "something."

From then on my life was destined by my responses to accidental events.*

I had to cut short a trip in the fall because the Lebanon French teacher had a nervous breakdown and they were desperate for a replacement.* I decided to accept his position (you did things like that in small towns).

Two years later I attended a reunion house party in Tennessee and took a stroll with my hostess's friend. During our walk I learned about her job with IBM which I envied, so she got me an interview with her boss.* Then, following many more interviews with "big shots," I landed the job. I worked in several different, interesting,

---

* Identifies "accidental events" throughout the story

challenging positions in Kentucky and Virginia and ended up in New York.

There an Episcopal priest, named Charles Fish, who knew of me through a mutual friend, called me at the office for a date.* (We couldn't get an apartment phone in those days.) After several calls to which I responded negatively (who wants to date a minister?), my cohorts dared me to check out the persistent fellow. I fell in love with him and we were married the following year, 1948, in July instead of October because he was offered and accepted a job in a church in Costa Rica in November.

We spent three years in San Jose, Costa Rica. We had so many interesting experiences and loved Costa Rica: the people, the climate, the food, the challenges, etc. We also welcomed two sons while there.

At first some locals assumed I was Charlie's "woman" since priests could not marry. Even the bank questioned accepting me as the wife of "Padre Fish." Charlie and I starred in a Little Theatre production which was held in the beautiful National Theatre. I was involved only because the leading lady got angry with her husband and flew back to the USA. I had attended the rehearsals so I knew most of the lines.

Costa Rica was very informal. I forgot to go to a luncheon given by the president's wife, so she called me and I dashed over in a "come as you are" outfit. She and her husband were very "down to earth" people.

We returned to Hamilton, Ohio, where we spent four years. It was a rather dirty town due to a paper factory there — seemed worse I'm sure after being in beautiful Costa Rica. Our delightful daughter was born in Hamilton.

The city was growing and had been mostly influenced by the factory, Champion Paper Company, located there for many years. It was interesting to watch the "old guard" people try to preserve their old customs in the face of the newcomers and modern ideas.

Our old rectory was considered marvelous by our older parishioners with no bathroom on the first floor, no kitchen cabinets, a gas leak in the basement, etc. (I put a child's potty chair in the kitchen to facilitate training.)

Contact by a friend of Charlie* resulted in an interview for him at St. Marks on the Mesa Episcopal Church and a move to Albuquerque, New Mexico, in 1956. (Charlie was rector there for 25 years.) On our first day, there was a dust storm and we couldn't see across the street! We moved around the city several times and enjoyed our neighbors wherever we lived. Especially we loved and appreciated the wonderful people at St. Marks who shared their lives with us – their joys, their sorrows and their love.

In the 1960s we built a little cabin in the mountains near Taos and really enjoyed summers up there. The children (each one usually bringing a friend along) were free to roam around, fish, swim, play golf and just play. Almost every day I played golf, too, and really loved it. The course was rather rustic, but beautiful.

When the children were off to college, I put my college education class learning to work and taught a few years at the Girls' Welfare Home, which was the penal institution for teenagers. I started as a "permanent substitute" and then was principal. Each of those girls faced severe challenges in their lives that were frequently the result of dysfunctional families. Working with them was a real privilege.

The rumor that being a clergy wife requires a conservative and pious life is completely untrue. My experiences have been unbelievably fantastic!

And didn't God have a hand in these "accidental" events? I am so grateful.

After Charlie's death I decided to "retire" at La Vida Llena. I still do a lot of community activities and LVL things, and have time to reminisce about a happy, exciting and blessed life.

Independence Early On
by
Miriam G. Friedman

My childhood in the Borough of Brooklyn, New York, was in many ways privileged. I had the opportunity to go to a small progressive private elementary school run by the Humanist Ethical Culture Society. And although I graduated 8th grade at 12½ years of age, I can remember by name and face all 20 fellow graduates.

The independence that was given me as a child allowed me to bicycle great distances from my home. Also, I was able to go by trolley or subway into Manhattan to attend theatre and participate in a choral group great distances from our home. I wonder whether youngsters today are allowed such independence with all the "crazies" lurking about at this time.

The opportunity to attend the college of my choice was given long before I graduated from a large public high school with an enrollment of some 4,000 students. I poured through college guides with utter abandon. Although I was only 16 at the time, I honed in on a very special liberal arts school in Ohio. Early admission to my first choice, Antioch College, in Yellow Springs, became a dream come true.

A special feature of the curriculum was a work-study program for each student. For my first job, begun in my second year of college, I was assigned to a job in Buffalo, New York, geared to parallel my focus of personnel service, now known as Human Resources. The second was Indianapolis, and little did I realize that this was to be the "turning point" of my life. It was there that the love of my life surfaced. I was then 18 and a young medical intern who became my partner for life charted the chapter that followed.

I was teaching at a private day school, and my students were prepared to give a presentation that night. In addition, a dinner dance was scheduled for us "young folks." Little did I know how my life would change that evening! A fellow house staff member of my future husband had two young women visiting from his home town and needed a blind date. Herb Friedman filled the position. The logical place for them to go was to the dinner dance at my school. We spotted each other, and so began our future life.

We married near the end of that year, 1953, and Herb and I moved to Chicago where he began his residency. After he "accepted" an offer to enter his choice of military service as a first lieutenant, choosing the Air Force, we moved to his assignment in Denver, Colorado.

We lived there for two years, my first experience of the West. We traveled through the Southwest and knew then we would ultimately live in this region. In 1958, after Herb completed his Urology residency in Baltimore, Maryland, we returned to the Southwest, choosing Albuquerque, New Mexico, to be our permanent home.

I was determined to pursue my college education. So after marriage I attended the Chicago Teachers College, which was what we could afford on a Resident's salary, as well as the salary I received working part-time for publisher, Houghton Mifflin. Ultimately I graduated from the University of Denver with a degree in education and my first child was born in Denver within months of my obtaining that degree. Not very long after, I had two more babies –

in all, three children all under 5 years of age. Today it seems impossible; I was all of 25 years old with three children. Those wonderful kids are now a doctor, a lawyer, and an engineer. When all three were well ensconced in school, I returned for further education, this time the University of New Mexico, and received a master's degree in Anthropology.

The direction of my life had changed when I headed to Antioch College and its unique program. The independence granted me early in childhood by my parents was a great gift given to an appreciative daughter. Ours was a close nuclear family, loving parents and a brother who became an academic achiever. I had been allowed to attend the college of my choice that in turn led to the wonderful journey that followed — a blessed marriage and family.

Our travels to all seven continents never ceased to diminish our desire to visit all corners of the world. Antarctica, with a one-on-one interface with its many varieties of penguins, seals, and ice was a true highlight. Even though we fearfully anticipated sailing through the Drake Passage (Herb has a serious problem with seasickness), the voyage passed without consequences.

The trip to Madagascar to view and even play with lemurs was a joy, but we did encounter a mild scare. One night Herb awoke with tachycardia while in a remote location, at least two days journey from proper medical treatment. Fortunately, he fell back to sleep and awoke without any problem.

Our journeys included visits to China, Easter Island, Iceland, Greenland, Yugoslavia (while it was one country), Timbuktu in Mali, Indonesia, Cuba, the five "Stans" (Uzbekistan et al.), Israel, Jordan, Morocco, Egypt, Saudi Arabia and the Arabian Emirates (we skied in Dubai), India, Japan, Viet Nam, Cambodia, as well as riding the Tran-Siberian Railway with a side trip to Mongolia, and touring many countries in Europe by bicycle.

All of these experiences occurred because I was allowed to be independent in my early years, i.e. to explore greater New York

City by bike and subway, attend theater and choral classes, and participate in sports. In young adulthood the confidence I achieved through earlier independent activities freed me to attend a unique college and make an adventuresome move to Indianapolis where I met the man of my life. All of this has given me a world of excitement.

WHY?

by
Kay Grant

I remember the moment well. Charlie — a visiting friend of my boyfriend, who was away on assignment — was sitting on the sofa, and I was sitting on the floor, leaning against a bookcase. "Katy," he said, "do you believe in God?" "OF COURSE!" I answered quickly and strongly.

"Why?" he asked quietly.

That understated word smashed into my brain with unimagined force. Why did I believe in God? I had never given it any thought. No one had ever asked me why I believed in God — more importantly, I had never asked myself. I believed but didn't know why.

I knew I could regurgitate things I had been taught in Sunday School, in the Christian youth groups I had belonged to, in the countless sermons I had heard, in the Sunday School lessons I had prepared and taught. But I also knew that wouldn't answer the question for me. I had to know — really know — why **I** believed, not what others told me I should believe.

How long did I sit there, staring at the carpet, my mind searching for an answer? It might have been 2 minutes; it might have been 20. Admonitions about going to hell if I didn't do this or that swirled through my mind. Meanwhile, Charlie never said another word. Finally, I looked up at him and said — in nearly a whisper — "because I'm afraid not to."

As the words tumbled out of my mouth, I knew that was not a good reason to believe and that I needed to find that reason within me. But never could I have imagined, as the stars twinkled in the sky over Germany, that I had taken the first step in what would become a decades-long journey.

I never saw Charlie again. He returned to his military duties, and I continued working for the U.S. Air Force in Germany and exploring Europe. A person who flitted into my life for a scant few hours had had a profound impact on my life and my thinking, and it all sprang from one little word — three little letters — that somehow awakened in me the desire to understand better, to find answers, not platitudes. *Why?*

It was not easy to turn away from something I had been taught since childhood, and I was afraid to abandon it easily, so I read some books on religion. A few years later when I settled in San Francisco, it was during an era of workshops, seminars, and classes on introspection, of delving into our souls, our minds, our psyches, to "find ourselves." None of these activities answered the *Why?*, but each, in some way, inched me forward on my journey.

I even took a theology class at the University of San Francisco — a Jesuit school — taught by a nun who seemed unable to answer questions from a room full of young, inquiring minds. That class, more than anything else, made me truly question the existence of God. There were no answers given to our questions; instead, parables were quoted, Bible stories proffered, and the admonition that we simply must believe without question. But how could I surrender my intelligence, my curiosity, my thirst to know, and just accept what someone told me to believe?

36

Life continued to parade through the years, and *Why?* returned to my consciousness time and again. *Why?* had found a permanent home in my brain cells and was diligently keeping itself alive.

In most cases, one's choice of religion is formed in childhood. One's home parish often is not a conscious choice but the following of family tradition. As I was growing up, it never occurred to me, nor would I have been encouraged, to attend another church, for even a single visit. Or to question my faith.

Faith is a deeply personal matter. I knew that many people throughout the world are taught that theirs is the one and only path to heaven (witness the many wars, skirmishes, battles, and terrorism, all in the name of Jesus/Allah/Buddha/Mohammed/other gods). I recognized that it is vital to the survival of any organized dogma that its followers be indoctrinated firmly in its teaching and beliefs and not question. The curious mind, however, seeks its own path. What are other doctrines like and how do they differ from what one is used to? Would I find the answer to *Why?* by exploring them?

A plethora of different denominations exist around the world, and at that time the San Francisco telephone book listed more than a hundred different religion subcategories.

A friend and I went on a pilgrimage to experience some of the different religious sects in the area—Swedenborgian; Jewish; a high Episcopal mass at the renowned Grace Cathedral; Buddhist; Church of Christ Science (in a beautiful Bernard Maybeck designed building); Seventh Day Adventists; the famous Glide Memorial United Methodist Church (with its charismatic preacher, Cecil Williams); Greek Orthodox; Church of the Latter Day Saints; St. Mary's Roman Catholic Cathedral (locally referred to as "the Bishop's Bendix" because of its architecture in a style resembling a washing machine agitator); Russian Orthodox; Unitarian; and others.

A fascinating adventure, but I didn't find the answer to *Why?*

At some point, decades after that fateful *Why?*, another defining moment shattered my thinking and woke me up, much like the earthquakes prevalent in the city where I chose to live shattered windows and set off car alarms. I suddenly realized that God and organized religion are two separate things. Two … Separate … Things. Why had I not seen that before? God doesn't need organized religion, but organized religion needs God or some master figure on which to hang its teachings, its guilt trips. By now I recognized that organized religions declare they are of love and forgiveness, but they teach guilt, fear, and punishment. "Do as we say, or you won't go to heaven."

To my mind, religion and spirituality are not synonymous. Simply put, spirituality comes from within, whereas religion comes from outside. The rules of organized religion are forced upon us and flow down from far away. They can be steeped in ritual, myth, mystery, or tradition; they are full of "cannots" and "shall nots," and they can be unforgiving of those who venture outside their confines (shunning, excommunication, etc.).

I feel that spirituality, on the other hand, follows an orbit of our choosing, flowing upward and outward from a belief (or desire to believe) in something larger than ourselves, that may have nothing to do with any organized creed.

While many people find organized religion comforting, others find its constraints artificially demanding and prefer to satisfy their souls in other ways. One may find solace in a sunset, peace in a pastoral setting, fulfillment in family and friendship. Music, mosaics, or memories may stir one's spiritual needs.

Or one may, as I did, turn away entirely from the spiritual experience, leaving behind the hypocritical teachings of organized religions and the super power/Godhead/mythological being.

I don't label myself an agnostic or an atheist. I am simply a nonbeliever in the teachings of the church I grew up in as well as other organized religious traditions. Nor do I want that God in my life — that "all-loving" being that allows children to be born deformed, addicted, or in poverty; that "all-powerful" being that allows earthquakes and tornadoes to strike innocent people; that "omnipotent" figure that permits people to languish in painful, consuming deaths.

Is there a God? I came to the comfortable conclusion that it doesn't matter to me. What matters is that I live my life my way and make my own decisions.

Why? is a traveling companion in all areas of my life. I am always asking *Why?* When I hear something new, unusual, needing clarification, or that I don't understand … *Why?*

My intellectual passport overflows with stamps of places I never would have visited without that *Why?* that resounded within me decades ago.

I never did find a reason to believe in God or to trust organized religions or those who follow their teachings without question. I did find reasons not to, however. And the journey was amazing.

Thank you, Charlie, wherever you are.

Me Do It
by
Jean Gregg

Who were the most influential people in my life? My parents! My mother Helen Bescherner was a very busy person who had little time to spend with me, especially after my brother, four years younger and sister, six years younger, were born. Not that I was ignored or neglected, but I was soon in kindergarten and was leading a more independent life. Anyhow, I was not especially interested in "babies."

I think I was born with an independent streak. My mother said some of my first words were, "Me do it." I never threw a temper tantrum. I did get sulky and would not speak to anyone until my better nature took over. My brother Arnold and I were "laid back," while my sister Irene was "high strung," and we got along fine.

My father Herman Bescherner, like my mother, was very busy. He owned a house painting and interior decorating business. He was able to keep about 15 painters working all the depression years — never missing a pay check. My mother kept the books. He retired when he was in his 80s.

We lived in the city of Cleveland, Ohio — far west side. It was the area for middle-class families with typical big city housing: narrow lots, two story houses with front porches, attics and finished basements.

My "playground" was the sidewalk "around the block." We were frequently told, "Don't play in the street. Don't cross the street. Be home in time for dinner."

From the second grade on, I walked to school on my own — no matter the weather! If I had homework, I was expected to do it. Since Mom often worked far into the AM doing the books, I dressed myself and got my own breakfast. My dad was the one who taught me to fry an egg.

My parents gave me a love for music. Mom was an accomplished pianist, could arrange music, was in the church choir, etc. My dad had a magnificent robust tenor voice! If he had not had terrible allergies that hit him every summer, he could have had a musical career — possibly opera — as his voice was of that quality.

Both belonged to the Archwood Methodist Church choir. After Friday night choir rehearsal, the director and the other members of the quartet, plus the director's husband, all gathered at 3503 Dover Ave. (our home) for a song fest. The director's husband had a wonderful baritone voice, and he and my dad made "the rafters ring." Glorious!

My love for animals and the outdoors came from my dad. He loved to hunt and fish. I was his tag-along shadow. I had my own .22 Rifle when I was 13. A few years later, I had my own Stevens single shot 410 shotgun. Not that I did much damage to wildlife: three squirrels, one hen pheasant who was eating in my strawberry patch.

My dad had hunting dogs: bird dogs, coon hounds and mixed breeds. I had my own cocker spaniel, Bootsie. Often there were puppies. Sheena, our Irish setter, raised 10 puppies in our basement, and Bootsie had six.

Another highlight in my formative years was Linwood Park on Lake Erie. My grandparents had a "cottage" there, and we Bescherner cousins spent many carefree summer days there. As soon as we were able to swim and follow some simple rules (no dunking, no throwing sand balls, and no going out over our heads), we spent as much of the day as we could on the beach. When we could swim a certain distance, my dad would allow us to swim the Vermilion River at the east end of our beach. There were two stone piers that guided the river into the lake, and that was where we swam.

We had, despite the fact that we were "city folks," farmer friends not too far from Cleveland, where I could roam, explore for hours with my dad, or be on my own.

There was not a lot of drama in my daily life. I do not remember my parents ever arguing. My dad was not a drinker.

I was not athletic. I liked to walk, hunt with my dad, swim, ride horses (they were "rental by the hour" animals), but I was not well coordinated for anything else! I think some of this was because I had had rheumatic fever when I was 8 years old. Bed rest was the only real treatment in 1932. I was six weeks flat on my back and six weeks getting back to normal. I was always the tallest in my class, and I think I grew 2 inches more during this illness. I lost a lot of muscle tone and gained weight. By the time I was 13 years old, I was 5 feet 8 inches tall and horribly overweight. I lost that extra poundage by the time I was 14 and grew no more.

I finished my years in public school in 1942. I loved most of my classes and did well, except for French! There was never any question about going to college. March of my senior high year I announced that I was going to go to Miami University in Oxford, Ohio — some 250 miles southwest of Cleveland. It was the oldest State University, had an excellent school of education and a fine arts department also. It was FAR from home! Being the first to leave the nest, I was sure I would be expected to come home often or would have unexpected guests who might interfere with my social life! Two hundred and fifty miles kept me on my own.

Despite WWII, my college years were wonderful. I majored in

art and history. I made lifelong friends there and graduated in 1946. My "me do it" spirit propelled me to accept a teaching position with the Department of Education in the Territory of Hawaii! My mother thought she would never see me again!

And so my real adult life began. Instead of one year on Kauai, I stayed 45. (I moved to Albuquerque in 1991.) I assured my mother the school was on high ground, and she did see me again and again. She made over 30 trips to Kauai.

I miss Kauai. But circumstances change and I have all the memories of life in Paradise. ALOHA

Midlife Decisions
by
Janet Hansche

When I was a child, my father told me that my mother was a Phi Beta Kappa, and I could probably achieve that honor too. My mother died when I was 10, but she continued to be a model for me. In those days, women typically did not work after they married. In the depression era, when jobs were hard to come by, employers preferred to employ men rather than married women. Career oppor-  tunities were limited. Thus, my mother, though she was a college graduate and had completed an internship in Dietetics, married my father and never worked professionally.

Dad wanted me to go to college and said he was prepared to pay for as much education as I wished to absorb. I went off to college expecting to fall in love and marry when I graduated. My expectations were fulfilled: the Education Department courses were interesting and well-taught, but the electives in liberal arts and the fine faculty who taught them were superlative. I graduated with high honors in Education and was elected to Phi Beta Kappa. I married my college sweetheart and began teaching first grade. But the marriage did not last.

I found that I was more interested in children with problems than in teaching and thus changed my focus from Education to psychology. Again, I did what I knew how to do: study hard and make good grades. I found many of the courses, both in theory and practice, very interesting. I married again, to a fellow Psychology student, who completed his Ph.D. I earned a master's degree in psychology but did not go on for a doctorate. Accidentally, I got pregnant, but the baby was born very prematurely and died.

We moved to New Orleans, and I became a Tulane University faculty wife. I enjoyed our life for a number of years. We lived in the university section of town and could walk to work. The children went to, reputedly, the best public school in town. Many of our friends were from faculty families. I worked part time as a counselor and was involved in the PTA and the Tulane University women's association. We were aware that many in our generation were having trouble in their marriages. This kind of difficulty became commonly referred to as a "midlife crisis."

I was shocked to discover that after less than 20 years of marriage my husband, Jay, told me that he was in love with another woman (younger, of course). I was in my 40s, had two kids in grade school and one in nursery school. How could I manage my life — and the children's lives? My father-in-law said it was all my fault, and I was glad that my parents were dead so that I did not have to tell them what a failure I was.

Once the shouting and the crying subsided, I began to figure out what to do. A friend recommended a good lawyer to handle a legal separation. My therapist helped me deal with my complicated feelings, including embarrassment that everyone would know that my husband had left me for another woman. At first, I just trudged along putting one foot after another to get through the day. I continued working as a counselor — aware that I had not been very successful in handling my problems. I reassured my children that their father loved them and would spend considerable time with them — which he did.

As time passed, life became more bearable. Because many couples our age were having marital troubles, I didn't feel like such a freak. I had a good friend who had recently gone through a divorce, and we began to do things together. Sailing had been a longtime pursuit in my family, and I suggested to my friend that she and I join the university sailing club. Eventually, we bought a boat that opened up a new social life. I met some men whose company I enjoyed. But there was no "prince charming" coming to my rescue.

I began to think about the future. The separation agreement was adequate to pay the bills, but my half of our former savings looked inadequate for the long run. While I was married, I was content to leave the career focus to my husband. Now the situation was different.

The Psychology Department at Louisiana State University (LSU) in Baton Rouge had just introduced a new program which allowed people who were working with a master's degree in Psychology to apply to their Ph.D. program without further entrance requirements. I think LSU made the offer to encourage people to aspire to the doctoral level. Throughout the country, a doctoral degree was strongly preferred for licensure as a Psychologist. Regardless of why the faculty offered it, the opportunity looked good to me. I made an appointment with the Chair, and he encouraged me to submit my transcripts and apply to the LSU program. Also, the Chair of Tulane University's Psychology Department urged me to pursue it.

There were roadblocks. LSU is about 80 miles from my home in New Orleans, a long daily commute. There were no doctoral programs in clinical or counseling psychology in New Orleans. I would have to quit my job and use some of my savings. I would have to seek more help with my children. I would have to study intensively for both the courses and the stiff comprehensives to follow. There was a dissertation to write and a year-long internship. Did I want to commit myself to this career? Although I was not exactly sure I could accomplish it, I felt that at last I was committed to pursuing the Ph.D.

To my surprise at just about this time, my husband said he wanted to "come home." We had been separated for about three years, and I had adjusted to being single. Of course, he had been in my life as the father of our children, and I was aware that I still found him more interesting than any other man I had known. I thought perhaps we could put things back together and have a future together.

But I did not want to give up my newly formed plans. Obviously, we would have to have a serious conversation, without the children around. Amazingly we could make that happen. The next day was the Friday preceding Mardi Gras. All of our kids had plans to stay with their friends over the weekend. I told them I was going to the beach in Florida with friends and gave them the phone number there.

Jay and I talked off and on over the weekend. I asked him to support me in my plans to return to graduate school. If he had opposed my plans, I would not have ended the separation. I had some very specific requests: to take charge of the family when I had to be in Baton Rouge for classes and other requirements and to take over most of the cooking and NOT complain. He agreed and kept his promise.

The whole process of getting the degree took pretty close to 10 years. I took an apartment near the LSU campus in which I stayed from Monday morning to Thursday afternoon and came home for the weekend. After a year or so, I gave up the apartment and lived at home with day trips to Baton Rouge as needed. We took family trips and vacations sometimes. One year I worked at the counseling center in the afternoons and on the dissertation in the mornings. I was lucky to get a U.S. Department of Veterans Affairs (VA) internship in New Orleans.

When I completed all the Ph.D. requirements, I applied for the position of Director at the counseling center where I'd worked so long. By the time I became Director, Jay was the computer guru in the Psychology Department at Tulane and a great cook. My daughter got married, my older son started college at Georgia Tech, and my younger son was in high school. I very much enjoyed the "career" I had postponed for so many years.

Quitting Was the Beginning
by
Illene M. Harrison

My life has had so many "turning points," it is difficult to decide which to discuss. So, I'll begin mid-way in my early life — my three children had reached their mid-teens, my husband and I had divorced after 15 years of marriage, and I was working in a management level job that I thoroughly enjoyed.

Way in the back of my mind I was considering moving to the Washington, D.C., area where pay scales were higher and I had many friends. Then one of the members of the Board of the business where I worked mentioned that his wife happened to visit the same beauty salon that both my boss's wife and I used. He went on to tell me that his wife told him that she had overheard my boss's wife say that she was going to have me fired because I was now divorced and should not be working in a management position any longer! Needless to say, I was not about to be fired from a position that I dearly loved and had held for several years. I immediately tendered my resignation, effective in one month.

After contacting my friends in Washington, D.C., I flew there and struggled through several job interviews. The interviews went well. It appeared I had a job with one of the federal agencies and I found an apartment I could afford (I thought). A couple of weeks later, the furniture was on its way to the Northern Virginia apartment and the three children, one cat, and I drove from South Dakota to Northern Virginia. While listening to the car radio in route, I heard that Congress had "frozen employment," and I wondered what that meant. Within days, the answer was all too obvious — the promised job no longer existed! After working as a "temp" for a while and being told by a man in an employment agency that they did not place women in management positions, I took a secretarial job to ensure that bills were paid. Over the next several years, my decision to move to D.C. paid off as I was able to change jobs several times — always to a better paying job and with advancement toward a management position.

In 1972, a director of the Federal Deposit Insurance Corporation (FDIC) needed a secretary. He was a political appointee and could hire his own secretary outside the Federal employment system. I happened to know some of the right people. I secured an interview, and they hired me. This job eventually morphed into an employee relations position at FDIC. While working there I earned a bachelor's degree (with honors) in business administration at Strayer University in Washington, D.C., and in 1974 I became a Certified Professional Secretary. All of this was accomplished through night courses while working full time.

Of particular interest at FDIC was that the bank examiners in the New York Region unionized and I was selected to work on management's team dealing with that new union — as well as several other unions that organized within FDIC during ensuing years. Fortunately, my children were very self-sufficient and took care of themselves without trouble because my job required extensive travel throughout the United States. This work was challenging and exciting to say the very least. And it moved me closer to my goal of securing a management position.

Ten years later I transferred to the U.S. Department of Agriculture in Washington, D.C. There I again dealt with labor organizations and gradually assumed responsibilities for employee benefits (health and life insurance and retirement benefits). In 1984, a law was passed making it mandatory that all federal employees, including members of Congress, be covered by Social Security. Congress then created a new retirement system for federal employees — the Federal Employees Retirement System (FERS) — and provided a six-month period when current employees could either stay with their current retirement plan, the Civil Service Retirement System (CSRS), or transfer to FERS. These changes created a tremendous need for training personnel specialists to determine which retirement system was best for each employee, as well as for newly hired employees who may or may not have had previous federal service. At that point, my labor relations functions were transferred to another person, and I became the Retirement Officer for the U.S. Department of Agriculture — a challenging and exhausting job, to say the very least. But I had arrived in the management world.

What a change that turning point in 1967 made in my life and that of my children. I was able to purchase a condominium. All three children successfully graduated from high school and went on to college. And the last 15 or so years of my career brought recognition for my management skills throughout certain sectors of the federal government.

By 1993, I had accumulated enough years to qualify for federal retirement benefits. Much to my surprise and pleasure, my retirement "party" was held in the USDA's auditorium in the Administration Building on The Mall. More than 100 colleagues, including the Department's Director of Personnel and the Assistant Secretary for Administration, attended. Who would have thought this could happen to a farm kid from South Dakota?

My son married and lived in Los Angeles, California; my oldest daughter also married and lived near Pittsburgh, Pennsylvania;

and my youngest daughter lived in Albuquerque, New Mexico. Although I had owned a condo in Northern Virginia for 17 years, it was obvious that I could not afford to remain there forever. So I scouted the country to decide where to live during retirement. Albuquerque's mild climate and affordable cost of living won hands down, and the move to the Southwest was another turning point in my life.

I flew to Albuquerque in January 1993, purchased a house, and moved in June of that year. At that point, the only person I knew in Albuquerque was my daughter!

Fortunately, I was invited to attend a Kiwanis luncheon meeting and soon became a member of that service organization. In 1999-2000, I was President of the Kiwanis Club of Albuquerque. Several years later I was honored to become President of the Southwest District of the Kiwanis Foundation. That gave me the opportunity to make many new friends in New Mexico, Arizona and Texas.

While performing volunteer service through Kiwanis, I helped children and young adults in a variety of ways. Helping children and young adults was something I had always wanted to do, but I had found it impossible due to job demands on my time and energy.

After 20 years of living in a lovely three-bedroom home in the Taylor Ranch community (that portion of Albuquerque existing west of the Rio Grande River), yet another turning point occurred in my life. My health was no longer robust, and it was obvious that I could no longer personally maintain my house and that lovely huge yard! So, after consulting with my children and others, I sold my home and am now a happy resident of La Vida Llena in northeast Albuquerque. Believe it or not, there are bridges spanning the Rio Grande, and I use them frequently! LVL is a wonderful place to live. I have gained many new friends but can still keep in touch with my Taylor Ranch friends as well as friends from the Washington, D.C., area.

The number and variety of turning points in my life have presented opportunities to learn new things and, of greater importance, to gain many, many friends ranging from South Dakota to Northern Virginia, Washington, D.C., and now Texas, Arizona and New Mexico. Life is wonderful, from turning point to new turning point. Believe it!

A Fallback Babysitter Gains a Family
by
Donna Roehling Hill

Marcie and Jerry Fitch came into my life when I was almost 16. They had recently moved to Denver when Jerry was appointed Rocky Mountain Bureau Chief for United Press.[1]

Marcie asked a neighbor for names of reliable babysitters. As I was only a fallback when their regular sitter was unavailable, I was a "safe" name to share while being a helpful good neighbor. Babysitting involved the care of two delightful children. Until I had my own children, 3-year-old Mike and 1-year-old Kathie were my favorites. The adults were also on a first name basis — directly opposite to the custom of that generation who expected teenagers to address all adults as Mister, Missus or Miss.

The family lived in a two-bedroom townhouse on the far east side of Denver. I had to experience Chicago traffic before realizing

---

1 In 1958, United Press (UP) merged with International News Services to form United Press International (UPI). (Verified: Associate Press Stylebook, 1980 edition.) Jerry Fitch was with UP before and after WWII until leaving in 1951 for KGLN.

that their drive to pick up a sitter on Denver's Southside was not a problem for former Chicagoans.

The Fitches were generous employers who always rounded up the sitting time, then added travel time to the total charge. Not like the woman who gave me half the going rate of 25 cents an hour. Her rationale: because I was working there for a full day, I would be earning more at 12½ cents per hour than if I were working only three hours at 25 cents per hour.

Both adults were out-going individuals who depended on an available sitter. Occasionally, I stayed overnight and slept on the couch. My parents never thought to set a curfew. Jerry needed to know and interact with the important people in his field and individuals who made things happen. Marcie, who had been in the entertainment world, was knowledgeable in many areas and a gracious hostess. It was she who bought me my first red dress to prove that I, a strawberry blonde, could wear red.

On the long ride home, Jerry listened to my dreams. I wanted to be a writer, but did not know how to proceed. College was my goal. How to get there was the problem. My parents were of no help. Neither had finished high school. Mother's employment skill was that of a comptometer operator, the predecessor of computers; Father had apprenticed the painting trade. Even if they could have afforded the tuition, my father did not believe in education for three daughters beyond high school. They would become just wives and mothers.

Eventually, Jerry took charge of our conversations. Mainly he talked about the newspaper world because that was his background. He raised my thinking from writing the "Great American Novel" to the practical side of making a living while doing what one liked and did best.

During my senior year, I worked on the school newspaper. I volunteered and was appointed to submit news articles to the Denver Post's High School section. It was Jerry's contact there who did him a favor by finding me a paid position: typist transcribing labor negotiations from a Dictaphone. When the Management/Labor agreement was reached, I moved on to spend the rest of my college years in different departments: Promotion, Retail Advertising and Library (the "Morgue" in newspaper jargon). In the 1950s, women, including me, were hired as typists and secretaries. The fortunate few on the staff of the Women's Page attended and reported on fashion shows and women's charity events.

The Promotion Department was set up to reward advertisers and government officials with train trips to Cheyenne Frontier Days (rodeo) and box seats at Denver sporting events. Both newspaper subscribers and non-subscribers could enjoy summer operettas staged on the outdoor Greek Temple in Cheesman Park. These and other events were targeted to promote the Denver Post within its distribution range.

College became possible with a combination of my part-time Denver Post job, a one-year University of Denver (DU) scholarship, part-time babysitting that included a high school graduation gift of a portable typewriter, and frugal living. After four years, I graduated with a degree in journalism and advertising.

At first the commute to DU was easy. Boarding the #8 streetcar (aka Tramway Tech) a block from home took me to the campus. However, my parents were having a house built in an adjacent town. When they moved, my route consisted of a local bus, a Denver bus, and that streetcar. A nightmare schedule! That was when I was invited to live with the Fitches. The arrangement included room and board plus pay for child care.

Marcie helped me grow into the woman I became. Her parents and an uncle owned shoe and women's apparel shops in Chicago. She brought back a suit that she knew would be a good choice for my growing wardrobe. Marcie gave me gentle lessons in how to relax and feel comfortable around others.

Late that spring, Jerry and Marcie announced that they would be moving to Glenwood Springs, Colorado, as co-owners and manager of KGLN radio station. Both would be on the regional airwaves with news and activities programs. Jerry's background included Armed Forces Radio in Japan — broadcasting south to the Philippines. Marcie, with her entertainment background and lovely voice, was a natural. Jerry was often on the road to convince business owners of the benefits in supporting their local station through their advertising.

Arranging for me to stay a month with a neighbor was their way of anticipating how the news of their move would affect me. After that transition, I found employment as live-in sitter for two other families.

These were not the easier times I had enjoyed with Marcia and Jerry. During my junior year, I returned to live with my parents. The commuting problem was solved because I was now able to afford a 1937 Chevrolet Coupe with rumble seat. There's truth in the statement, "You can't go home again." My parents had found that the cost of mortgage payments, utilities and home insurance on their new home greatly exceeded those of that small old duplex's low rent. I was expected to contribute toward the increased grocery cost.

Marcie and Jerry continued to support my emotional needs. During school holidays, I traveled on the California Zephyr to their mountain home. After I graduated and moved to Chicago, we continued to exchange gifts for a few years. We never lost touch. Christmas times always included notes or letters about what each family had accomplished that year.

In the days before computer-generated type, information was transcribed through a series of mechanical processes to become printed news. The Denver Post hired John Hill, a graduate mechanical engineer, to assist the Purchasing Agent. John's primary assignment was to purchase technical materials for maintaining the printing equipment.

60

Before we married, the Fitches met and approved of John. When we drove a dealer's Mustang to California, we visited the Fitches in Glenwood Springs. On a trip to Mesa Verde with our two children and a niece, we stopped in Durango — where they had moved after purchasing radio station KDGO.

In 1999, after considering other retirement locations, John and I moved to Albuquerque. By then, Marcie and Jerry could be found in Scottsdale, Arizona. Our vacations with Elderhostel included two programs in Arizona. At the conclusion of these events, we stayed on to visit with other friends and especially with Marcie and Jerry. We enjoyed meeting their adult daughter Kathie, who had worked for three radio stations in Colorado and a TV station in Denver. After her move to Scottsdale, Kathie joined major department stores where women's casual clothes and swimwear were her specialties. Marcie added her observation: our Mike and Kathie are each 20 years older than your Steve and Nancy.

Our last trip to Scottsdale in 2007 was a sad one. Marcie's memorial service was held in the clubhouse of the community where they lived. The informal reception was a charming, low-key gathering for family and friends. Marcie would have approved.

There we met Mike, his wife, two daughters and two grandchildren. As an expert in wireless and satellite telecommunication, Mike worked as an attorney and in executive positions with the FCC, the U.S. State Department, private corporations, and as CEO of an international trade association for wireless telecommunication infrastructure companies. Both Kathie and Mike had followed the family interest in communications.

When Jerry died in 2013, we were unable to attend his memorial service. Mike sent us the newspaper articles that reported the many accomplishments of his father's life. Mike has continued his parents' communications with us through email. We now exchange Christmas letters. Kathie is also on our email list.

I was privileged to know these people for 65 years. Marcia and

Jerry were my friends and mentors. They made all the difference in my life.

On one of our last visits, Jerry commented that they enjoyed finding waifs and helping them get a start. At the time, I was somewhat taken aback at this description. However, his was the observation of a reporter who carefully chose words to briefly tell a story. It took me time to realize what I was when found. What I became in my life received their recognition and approval.

My Life as a "UU" (Unitarian Universalist)
by
Marilyn W. Hill

It was the spring of 1967. I, recently widowed, had moved to Albuquerque with my two young daughters the previous summer. We were living in a house on Palo Duro Street and working at building a new life in a new town. I was beginning what would be a 22-year teaching career with the Albuquerque Public Schools. The girls — Jennifer and Janet, ages 10 and 8 — were busy with school, music lessons, and Girl Scouts.

As so often happens in Albuquerque in the spring, we were experiencing a period of windy weather. On this particular day the wind was especially strong, so papers were being blown about up and down the street, with a fair number being caught in my front yard rosebushes. When I went out to clean the yard, one of the papers I found was an order of service from the First Unitarian Church, which was located just a couple of blocks away. My interest was piqued by what I read, so I decided to go there the following Sunday to check it out.

From that very first attendance, I felt such a sense of community, such a sense of being at home, that I very quickly signed the

63

membership book. I enrolled the girls in Sunday school, which they attended right through high school. My daughter, Janet, was the youngest member of the church when she died at age 19. And I am pleased that Jennifer has raised her children in UU churches in the various communities where she and her family have lived.

Around 1970 our UU church instituted an Extended Family program, the rationale being that since most church members did not have real-life family living nearby, this would promote a sense of closeness with a small group within the church. The families were intergenerational. Our family, the First Cousins, consisted of an older couple (the "grandparents"), a few single adults, and several families with children ranging in age from teenagers down to infants.

We shared holiday meals and many other activities, which, in the early days, were often child-centered. As the years passed, the "grandparents" died, some of our families moved away, children grew up and left home, and new adult couples joined us; so our focus shifted to more adult-oriented pursuits. Countless dinner parties ensued, as well as many driving trips to points of interest in New Mexico and other parts of the Southwest. For several years, we enjoyed an annual camping trip to the headwaters of the Rio Grande in Colorado. Only a few of us are left, and we no longer meet officially, but we remember our First Cousins days with fondness.

In the early 1970s, the growing number of single adults in the church led us to form a new group providing an opportunity for some intellectual stimulation and socializing. This group would be called by the rather "highfalutin" name, the Sunday Salon for Singles.

So for 13 years, I spearheaded a monthly get-together for from 30 to 40 people. We met in people's homes (mostly mine). The meeting began with a speaker from the community (UNM faculty were a great resource). Our topics were far-ranging. One notable example was a debate between gubernatorial candidates (one of whom had lost his voice from over-campaigning), and another was a talk by representatives of the local Naturist Society (they arrived fully clothed). The program was followed by dinner that, with a few trusty helpers, I shopped for, cooked and served. After some time, we were able to come up with a workable schedule for our menus — sort of an "if it's November it'll be lasagna" system. The Sunday Salon required a lot of work and planning, but it was satisfying and much appreciated by the attendees.

On the last Sunday in April of 1977, I had arrived early at church when I noticed a gentleman whom I had not seen before and who appeared to be a newcomer, so I decided to greet him. In later years, he always liked to tease me by saying that I "pounced" on him, but I felt that I was very genteel in welcoming him to our church. He was, indeed, a first-time visitor and had recently returned to his childhood home of Albuquerque after retiring from a long engineering career in California. It so happened that I had an extra ticket for a church spaghetti supper scheduled for that evening. It seemed a shame for it to go unused, so I invited him to go with me. He asked me to dinner later that week, and upon his arrival at my house to pick me up, he noticed a small electrical problem, which he offered to repair. Of course, I had to invite him for dinner as repayment — and the rest, as they say, is history.

Since Ken was already retired, he had time to become quickly involved in volunteer projects at church, including helping me with Sunday Salon chores. And, when Janet was diagnosed with melanoma later that year, he was my source of emotional strength, as well as the provider of practical help. I've often said that I could not have made it through her illness and death without him beside me.

After what was probably one of the longest courtships on record (17 years), we eloped to the Tippecanoe County Courthouse in Indiana and were married in September of 1994. Seventeen more happy years followed until Ken's death in 2012. The UU church was a constant presence in our life together.

When I retired from teaching in 1987, I joined the church CARE Committee, which provides needed help and support to fellow church members. I soon became the official card sender. Over the years I have written hundreds of notes of congratulations, condolences, concern during illness — whatever the needs may be.

For the past several years, I've been part of a group comprised of seven UU women. We meet monthly to catch up on each other's life and for dinners, concerts, or other events of interest. Our association with each other has been a source of support and close friendships that are very dear to me.

Shortly after Ken and I moved to La Vida Llena retirement community in 2008, two fellow UU residents and I, in collaboration with First Unitarian's minister, formed a satellite group to meet at La Vida Llena to accommodate UU residents and other likeminded folks. Ministerial interns from First Unitarian have served as facilitators for our twice-monthly meetings at which we watch a video sermon by one of First Unitarian's ministers and participate in a lively discussion. After six years our group is flourishing, and we expect this to continue into the foreseeable future.

So ... was it an act of Providence as some have suggested? Or was it just a random gust in that spring windstorm that delivered that particular piece of paper to my rosebush on Palo Duro Street? Whichever it was, it was the event that has helped to shape my life for these past 47 years — a life that has been happy and fulfilling.

A Goal Achieved
by
Charleyrene Hines

My parents worked on a ranch in West Texas. When the time came to have their first baby, they got into their buggy and drove from the ranch to the Silvers farm in New Mexico. They picked up Sallie Silvers, my grandmother, to accompany them to the Portales Hotel in Portales, New Mexico. The three adults conferred with a doctor who came to the hotel to supervise my birth on January 30, 1922. I was named Charleyrene after my mother's favorite brother Charley.

Sallie Silvers returned to her farm home and the new parents, Howard and Lydarene Rogers, returned to the West Texas ranch where they worked. I grew up over the next few years and could walk a half block from my home to the home of my grandparents, Jim and Sallie Silvers, in Littlefield, Texas.

Soon the family, including me and my younger sister, moved to Albany, Texas, for a short time before settling in Bledsoe, Texas, where we attended school. Then the family moved to the Rogers Ranch in eastern New Mexico where in 1939 we graduated from a small country high school in Lingo, New Mexico.

As far back as I can remember COLLEGE was my goal. My mother always regretted that she could only go to school through the eighth grade, and she wanted more for her daughters. I heard the message loud and clear.

Times were hard in eastern New Mexico and West Texas. There was no extra money. However, I earned a scholarship to Eastern New Mexico University (called Eastern) in Portales, New Mexico, and had the opportunity to work at the school. So I was able to get started toward my dream. The second year my mother asked her brother (after whom I was named) if he could help with my college and he sent me a monthly check to help with my expenses. I studied business — typing and shorthand and all that was needed to be a good secretary. I liked it very much, and that continued to be the focus of my education and later my teaching.

After my second year at Eastern, my favorite teacher and mentor, Dr. Sharp, recommended me for a program that was sending 30 students from Eastern to Washington, D.C., to work for the government. It was exciting to be chosen, and we all had big expectations. I worked in a typing pool doing work for government offices.

However, the big city was not for me. I felt out of place with strange people. My mother was a very good seamstress and had sewn me a lovely wardrobe of clothes that I liked very much, but I felt others made fun of me. I was homesick and missed Fred Danforth, the boy I had dated since high school. I decided to go back to Portales.

That decision set the course for the rest of my life. I think my life would have been quite different had I stayed in Washington, D.C. I have been very happy in my New Mexico/Texas homes.

When I returned to Portales, I could not afford to go back to college. I taught in a one-room school house on a ranch for several months, then in White Sands, New Mexico. Fred and I decided to marry and work together toward our college education — my field was business, and Fred's was music. We shared the goal of complet-

68

ing college, and it shaped our entire life together — over 30 years.

Fred took a job in California, and we moved there until our first child was born. We moved back to Portales, lived in married student housing at Eastern, and continued taking classes. Fred got his degree in Music and took a band director job in Morton, Texas. We had two children so I took care of them, worked when I could, and took college classes when I could.

It was a big day when I graduated with a bachelor's degree in Business from Eastern New Mexico University in 1944. My parents and sister came to graduation. I was so happy that they had come and that I had achieved my goal of COLLEGE.

My detour to Washington, D.C., had not changed me, but my decision to return to New Mexico and pursue college had. I was now a qualified High School Business teacher. I had worked hard and made it! I had a role in life; I enjoyed my students; I helped make a living for our family.

Fred and I taught in the same schools most of the time. I continued my pursuit of college by getting a master's degree and took other advanced education classes — even driving to Las Cruces to attend summer classes at New Mexico State University. Fred was the much-loved band director. We were still teaching at Texico High School, Texico, New Mexico, when he died from cancer in 1988.

I still enjoy attending the Texico homecomings. At the 2014 Homecoming, a former student came up to me and said, "I remember you, you are my typing teach." I had achieved my long-dreamed of goal — a college education. That education opened to me a career as a teacher. Being remembered by a student after all these years is just one of the many wonderful consequences.

Finding Feminists — World Wide
by
Louise Hodell

In the 1960s and 1970s my involvement in feminist activities in New York City seemed to prepare me for an easy adjustment to living and working in a new country later. How could that be?

Then I thought about my mother Elsie. All during my childhood and youth she introduced me to aspects of feminism and women's issues, such as discrimination and outright exclusion from employment in many career paths open to men, equal pay for women and men doing the same work, and the weakness of rape laws, to mention a few.

When these and similar subjects came up in the popular press of those days, she would talk to me and my sister about the unfairness of current employment practices and the now public concept of a "glass ceiling." In many lines of work, a woman had to resign from her job if she got married, even school teaching jobs. My grandfather, Elsie's father, took a strong vocal stand against married women working. They were supposed to stay home, bring up children, and always be available to help their husbands. Their lifetime role was simply to be a great housewife and mother, etc., etc.

Many years later, Elsie's counsel and frequent discussions made it easy for me to accept and avidly join feminist activities. Topics like consciousness raising, reading the exploding new literature about women's concerns, attending meetings and conferences led by organizations like the National Organization of Women (NOW) were not only easy for me to understand, but actually to seek out. They fitted the frame of mind Elsie had given me. She had presented women's issues as comfortable to think about and needing public expression and legitimate personal attention.

Although she never lived to see how her family conversation colored my later life in many positive ways, she had prepared me well to welcome the newly revived Women's Movement in the 1970s.

Her words also helped me in other ways. Later I was recruited to teach in a college overseas. The position would be in the field of teacher preparation. I saw it as an opportunity to promote another lifelong direction: personal, professional growth and expansion of skills.

My two sons had grown up, graduated college, and were young adults entering their career paths. They did not object to my going to Australia to work. Some family and friends questioned the decision — "Are you going all alone?" "Do you have friends there?" "That's far away, isn't it?" (Actually it's on the other side of the earth from New York City. A knitting needle stuck through the middle of a globe shows Perth, Australia, at the opposite side from New York City.)

During my earliest weeks after arriving in Perth, I discovered a newspaper notice about an upcoming meeting of the Women's Electoral Lobby (WEL). It turned out to be almost a cousin of our National Organization of Women (NOW).

I attended the meeting, was introduced to the audience, and later that afternoon was invited to dinner at the home of the membership chairperson. The group, gathered in a church room, was discussing many of the same concerns I had heard in USA meetings. It all sounded familiar. From that moment on, WEL provided me a ready-made community of thoughtful, politically aware women. They took me over the years to conferences, lectures, discussion groups; and taught me about women's issues in that country. They introduced me to local dramatic presentations, concerts, elections, and many other aspects of their national culture.

I began to see Australia as having many similarities to our own USA history: early British colonial government, social discrimination, an Anglo-European approach to construction of the legal system, not to mention our common language and literature base, approach to general welfare, and much more. Without the comforting social support and friendship of the WEL group, it might have been much more difficult for me to enjoy my new teaching position.

Much later several of the friends I met at WEL activities were voted into state and federal positions. Their combined efforts rested in Australia's adoption of numerous laws having to do with equal rights, much before we in the USA defeated such efforts as our Equal Rights Amendment (ERA).

Soon after my arrival in Australia, I was invited to join a delegation of WEL members who were to "lobby" their senator to the national parliament. We were to politely remind him of our push to pass equal rights laws in Australia. It turned out he was more interested in querying me about current efforts at that time in the USA to pass legislation supporting care and upbringing of severely handicapped infants and children. Policy related to handicapped infants and children was a subject I knew something about because only a few years earlier I had completed six years directing a program for birth defect babies and toddlers in New York City. It was flattering that he wanted my opinions. Services and care of the handicapped are certainly tangential to women's issues — women do much of that work.

Since class assignments were only pending at the new college that hired me, another unusual opportunity was suggested to me: review outback rural schools and special children's programs. With another "lecturer" (Australian word for a college teacher) I went by bus to Carnarvon on the Pacific Ocean coast, north of Perth. We visited a nursery/kindergarten program in an aboriginal community (something like Indian reservations in the USA).

The program was a government effort to expand pre-elementary schooling down to the children's earliest years of life — another common concern of our two countries, much discussed in public and educational circles and closely related to women and family issues. The school room, in a small wooden house, was furnished as any good kindergarten with a doll corner, block building corner, book reading area, small tables and chairs for making puzzles and later for eating snack.

Collected outside the front door were several aboriginal mothers each holding a toddler in one hand and an infant in the other. They leaned into the doorway, peering carefully at us inside. The children, like most 3 and 4-year-olds, gravitated eagerly to the shiny new toys inside. The morning went well. The two regular teachers supervised children's free play, showed and read picture books to them, sang with them (mostly TO them) well-known children's songs.

One unique experience I had at Carnarvon was a visit to watch a radio program called Kindergarten of the Air. A tiny office at the local radio station broadcast this program designed for children living on isolated sheep stations (read: American ranches). The teacher, from a local kindergarten, used two foot pedals under her desk plus a microphone and other electronics on the desk to call far-flung sheep stations, one at a time, usually at the station manager's home. Because of the vast distances separating children of the same age, these students probably had few other playmates — not enough to support a school.

It was charming to overhear the children's tiny voices answering the teacher's questions, describing some event of interest at their station since the last week. Worksheets, children's books, materials suitable for their tender age were sent weekly by mail. That is, dropped in a bag from an airplane (!) — the only postal service available to these widely separated locations. It impressed me, the lengths to which the Western Australian government went to overcome the educational void experienced by young preschool children living with parents working on the stations.

One unfortunate effect of the remoteness of the sheep stations was that "distance learning" was not available to all and many older children were sent away to boarding schools in towns with larger populations. Still of tender age, they had to live away and only see their families during vacations.

What I saw of schooling in Australia 45 years ago may have led to changes today. Perhaps the advent of computers means faster and more thorough communications for more students today. Distance learning is also a concern of educators in the USA — another example of common cultural concerns in our two countries (and many others).

To end on a lighter somewhat comic note, let me include an incident, commonly occurring between our two countries. While living and working in Australia just after their big national election, a representative of the "shire" (something akin to our "county") knocked on my front door, clipboard in hand. He wanted to know why I had not voted in the recent election. Graciously he accepted my explanation that I was still a citizen of the USA and thereby, forbidden to vote in his country. This explanation had a good result — I avoided the five pound (about $25 US) penalty for not voting and possibly legal complications for me!

The years I spent working in that country and especially the friendship I made among the members of the Women's Electoral Lobby leave warm and respected memories in my heart. And without Elsie's preparation of my heart, soul, and mind, it might have been much more difficult for me to so quickly and easily accept the newly burgeoning ideas of a revived women's movement in the 1970s.

My sense of community with women of this world has grown. My sense of self and national and world developments has expanded. It has engendered my sense of well-being and satisfaction and appreciation of my place in this 21st century life. So … Thank you, Elsie. Thank you, World-Wide Women's Movement. Thank you, Australia and the women of the Women's Electoral Movement. You all have played a deep and appreciated role in my life.

The Importance of Parents
by
Marian B. Hoge

On a day in March 1930, there was a knock on the door of our second-floor flat in Springfield, Massachusetts. Mother opened the door to find two white-coated persons, a man and a woman. They quickly announced that she (Mother) was to get her coat and come with them. Mother protested that she could not leave the children (four of us) unattended. They assured her that the woman downstairs would look after us.

Things were to change drastically again when my father remarried 2½ years later. My stepmother was a very well educated woman with a master's degree in English and experience as a high school teacher. She had also spent two years teaching English in a Negro college in Mississippi. Education was very important to her and her goal was for each one of us to go to college. However, her commitment to equality for Negroes and where that took all of us became, perhaps, the most significant influence in my life.

The depression descended on us one year after my dad remarried. For one year my dad worked for the Works Progress Administration (WPA) and my stepmother, now Mother, worked for the

Public Works Administration (PWA) as she was a professional. We lived with grandparents who owned a large house. In time, my dad was able to get a job with the Department of Agriculture in their Boston offices. We lived in Concord, Massachusetts, for the next five years through my first year of high school.

When my dad was transferred to Chicago, Mother insisted that we had to live in Winnetka, Illinois, where the schools were supposed to be the best in the nation at that time. Winnetka is an affluent North Shore village 16 miles north of downtown Chicago. Though we were not affluent, we settled there, and we girls had to cope with the economic differences among the students at New Trier High School. The school was an integrated public high school with a large number of Black students, mostly from newly professional families. However, the racial groups, as well as the economically different groups, were quite stratified. My sister and I enjoyed the music and dancing of the Black students during lunch hour. We learned about racial and economic divisions and struggled with finding our "place." I, in keeping with my family's values, thought it was good to have such variety at our school.

Mother was also looking for opportunities to return to the interracial work she had done in the past. She spoke to a librarian at the Evanston library who told her that the only people doing interracial work in the area at that time were the Quakers. Oddly enough Mother was not aware that Quakers even existed anymore. Upon learning what the Quakers were doing, Mother announced that we would be attending the Friends (Quaker) Meeting in Evanston on the following Sunday.

The Friends families represented an economic cross-section of the community and found common values and interests separate from their financial positions. My sister and I began attending the Friends teenage group which met Sunday evenings. The young people had liberal ideas and were from families who lived out that line of thinking. It was easy for us to talk with these kids. Mother told us that the Friends Meeting was an opportunity to know "affluent" people who thought the way we did. We found that to be so and enjoyed the youth activities, as well as meeting.

Yet another change took place near the end of my junior year when my dad was transferred to Washington, D.C. During the middle of my senior year, the family would be moving to a permanent home on the outskirts of D.C. In order to avoid another change of high schools, my younger sister and I were shipped off to the Friends (Quaker) boarding school in Barnesville, Ohio. There we were to learn the thinking and life-style of the most conservative Friends — a big change from suburban Chicago!!

In Ohio many Quaker elders wore "plain dress" — the men wore dark, collarless coats and whenever outside the home wore black hats (even at meeting); women wore long, simple dresses, bonnet-type head coverings, and black shoes and stockings. At the boarding school, we learned much more about the values and practices of the Friends. Having come from a suburban environment to this rural community, we faced many changes, but we shared many values and felt welcome.

Following high school graduation, I went two years to Guilford College, a Quaker college north of Greensboro, North Carolina. It was wartime (1942-1944), and the news from Europe was quite depressing. It was not an inspiring time! My interest was in psychology, but the curriculum looked too daunting! I had no real goal in mind.

After these two years of college I decided to marry a young man I had met at the Friends Meeting in Washington, D.C. Even though he was a Quaker, my parents were dismayed that I was not finishing college. He was an Iowa farm boy from a very conservative Quaker background. He had a job in a local machine shop making parts for various kinds of machinery. Later he was working at Johns Hopkins Applied Physics Laboratories as a machinist when his boss announced he was taking a job in New Mexico and would be hiring people willing to make a move. To me it looked like an opportunity to leave the D.C. area which was crowded, expensive and very humid! My husband accepted the job.

In preparation for this huge move and wanting to have a connection in our new location, I checked with our Friends Meeting to learn if there might be a meeting in Albuquerque. I obtained the name and phone number of a Philadelphia Friend who was organizing a meeting in Albuquerque. Santa Fe already had a meeting organized by an Indiana Friend.

As time went on the Albuquerque Friends Meeting took a great deal of our time and attention. This diverse and loving community became the core of our life. A Quaker community is held together by the belief that God is in every person, a commitment to treating every person with respect, and taking care of the less fortunate. These have become my life-long values, and I discovered them through my mother's search for a community in tune with her interest in promoting education with the Black community.

Our Albuquerque Meeting grew slowly and in time we had satellite meetings in Las Cruces and Gallup, New Mexico, and Amarillo and El Paso, Texas. We met annually with Arizona Friends and in time organized our own Intermountain Yearly Meeting that also included Colorado and Utah Friends.

The founder of the Albuquerque Friends Meeting, Totsie Korn, was a very close friend. When she became ill, she came to me and said, "Marian, please take care of our meeting." I have tried to do that to the best of my ability. I am still in touch with her daughter. The love and support of many Friends in the Friends Meeting have made an indelible imprint on my life.

When our children became school age, I began to consider work outside the home. First I took a civil service exam and quickly found employment. The work, however, was very repetitive, and I soon realized there was no way I could stay with that job for 10 or a dozen years until the children were through college.

That meant serious consideration of a college degree which, of course, the quest for had been instilled in me by my mother long ago. I enrolled at the University of New Mexico in the fall and took some classes that semester. My goal at this point was to get a counseling degree which meant at least two years of teaching before I could apply for entrance to the graduate school. I taught elementary (fifth and sixth graders) at A. Montoya School in the canyon east of Albuquerque for 3½ years plus one year in the junior high teaching math. I was admitted to graduate school for the 1975-1976 year. In the fall of 1977, I began a counseling position at Washington Middle School in Albuquerque and worked with excellent students and staff. I very much enjoyed the work.

Throughout my life, my mother's influence has stayed with me whether it was to speak in a well-modulated voice or to be more responsive to those around me. I have also been blessed with wonderful children and grandchildren and now great-grandchildren!!

New York, New York!
by
Shirley Houston

It was the spring of 1954, and I was finishing my freshman year at Oklahoma A&M in Stillwater, Oklahoma. I was a regular in the Presbyterian Student Sunday School Class where the minister to students, Bob Geller, often focused on how our faith should alert us to the injustices in our society. The civil rights movement was beginning to be a regular news item — Brown v. Board of Education,  the unanimous Supreme Court decision striking down separate but equal schools, had been handed down in May.

Bob realized that the first step to successful integration was getting to know people of other races. He not only arranged for us to help with a clean-up project at a local black church and to attend services there, he also made sure we knew about church-sponsored summer work that would take us out of our comfortable, middle class, all-white world.

One of these was a program sponsored by the New York Mission Society — an old organization that had long worked with underprivileged kids in New York City. It was a summer work project that involved using white college students and other young people from all over the United States to serve as day-care workers in the poorer sections of Harlem and other depressed areas of the city. They would work side by side with black college students from the neighborhoods. The work project would serve the dual purpose of helping white and black students to get to know one another, as well as provide a service to neighborhood families. As an added incentive, New York City Mission Society would arrange for us to see several Broadway plays, eat at ethnic restaurants once a week and generally enjoy the cultural life of the city with our coworkers throughout the summer. Those of us from outside the city would live together in the bell tower of the Broome Street Tabernacle on the Lower East Side.

I was hooked — I must admit the lure of living and working in New York City was probably more compelling than working with the children, but I was idealistic and saw myself as doing a good deed while having a really good time!

My next job was convincing my dad back home in Texas that it was an experience that I could not miss. He very sensibly would have liked for me to work at a paying job to help with college expenses. He finally agreed, and a few weeks later I boarded the train in Dallas for the two-day journey. Two University of Texas students were also going, and we arranged to meet at the train station. A sleeping car was much too expensive, so we were riding in the chair car section. When traveling in 1954 one dressed in her Sunday best — hat, gloves, the complete ensemble. I don't remember much about the trip except that my feet swelled in my high heel pumps during the night so I took them off only to discover I couldn't get them back on the next morning! I also remember waking up as the train was following the Hudson River near West Point — all that greenery and water was quite a sight for a Texas Panhandle girl.

We came into Grand Central Station and caught a cab to Broome Street that would be our home for the summer. I was smitten — I loved the noise, the fast pace, even the smells! We were greeted by M. Alice Towne, a handsome, grandmotherly woman who was to be our guide, mentor, housemother and friend during our weeks here. Her first assignment was for us to learn to use the subway system. She handed us a subway map and sent us out to try our luck — Miss Towne did not believe in pampering.

I was assigned to Harlem River Houses to work with preschoolers. Another Broome Street girl, Martha, a second-grade teacher during the school year, was to be with older children there. So off we went to Harlem to meet our co-workers. When we arrived at 155th Street, a baseball game was about to start at the nearby Polo Grounds, and a big Irish cop thought we were trying to find our way to see the Giants play. When he offered to help us, we asked for directions to Harlem River Houses. He told us in very strong terms to get back on the subway and go back where we came from. This was our introduction to Harlem.

We eventually did find Harlem River Houses, a huge WPA housing project built during the 1930s. Our classrooms were in the basement meeting rooms of two separate buildings. We found our co-workers there — Betty Brewington, a freshman at Virginia Union, was to work with me. I liked her immediately — she was gracious, warm and wonderfully accepting of this do-gooder from Texas. "Miss Betty" had been raised in "The Projects" and her family still lived there. She had a contagious laugh and a great sense of humor. She would need it often during the summer of 1954 while educating her naive white co-worker from Texas, "Miss Shirley."

After a short orientation, we started to work. We had about 15 kids on a regular basis who were with us from 9-3. The children were a wondrous mix — gentle Mention whose huge brown eyes peered through tiny wire-rimmed glasses; tough Roxanne who reeked of urine and was the self-appointed group leader; immaculate little Puerto Rican dolls, Frankie and sister Marie, delivered each morning by their hugely pregnant mother; sweet little Butter so nicknamed because of his lovely color. Each noon we walked the children about a block to PS 90 where they were served sack lunches. After lunch, we watched as they played on the playground outside our classroom. The little girls clapped out intricate rhythms — "Miss Mary Mack, Mack Mack all dressed in black, black black …" or jumped rope with precision and skill. Several times a week we took field trips with the kids, shepherding them onto the subway to visit Central Park, the Bronx Zoo, Jones Beach or the Statue of Liberty. Although I always worried that we would lose a child or one would tumble onto the subway track, nothing dire ever happened.

One day about mid-summer, Betty mentioned that she and her family were driving up to Camp Minisink to visit her brother. Camp Minisink was a facility run by New York Mission Society so city kids from poor families could have a camp experience. She thought I might like to see it and invited me to ride along. I took the subway up to Harlem early Sunday and met Betty's family. They were all cordial except her father — I was mystified by his coolness.

It was the beginning of a long learning process for me. Betty and the parents of our preschoolers had so readily accepted me that I had naively assumed that they all thought I was wonderful for giving my summer over to working in Harlem. In time I would come to understand why a black father might feel uncomfortable as a white woman from Texas intruded on his Sunday outing with his family. He had perhaps had experience with the Jim Crow laws — separate water fountains and other humiliations so common in Texas at that time. Nevertheless, I was treated with courtesy and had a good time. I also realized for the first time how it felt, if even for just one day, to be a minority — I did not see another white face all that day.

Sometimes when I was supervising the playground in Harlem, a young black man who lived in "The Projects" would come over and visit with me. He was a college student about my age, and I enjoyed our conversations. One day he mentioned that his family

86

would be driving through Texas soon and wondered if they would be able to find a place to stay in Amarillo, a town near my home. I assured him that there were lots of motels in Amarillo, and they wouldn't have any trouble at all. In my ignorance and insensitivity I had given him a very incorrect answer. He knew, of course, that I would not have trouble finding a room. He was asking if a black family would find accommodations. Again, I was just beginning to realize that my experiences could not possibly tell me what it was like to live as a black person.

As time went on I gradually became more and more aware of the racial injustices that existed in every aspect of American society. But the larger lesson I began learning from my amazing summer in Harlem is that I must really listen to those whose life experiences are very different from mine. They have lived it; I have not. This journey of discovery started with "Miss Betty" in Harlem in 1954 and continues even now 60 years later.

Marcia's Story
by
Gerald Hunsberger

Marcia tutored Myungsoon Ma, a South Korean, from March 17, 2011, to April 2012. Her student, born in 1971, was married to a South Korean who spoke English and worked at Sandia Laboratories as a scientist. They parented three children ages 2, 7 and 11. Myungsoon possessed a Korean college undergraduate degree in electrical engineering.

My wife, a retired teacher, wanted to tutor after learning about a friend in Española, New Mexico, who was tutoring for pay. But, Marcia chose to donate her time rather than to earn money. She found this tutoring very satisfying because it enabled her to help someone who appreciated and needed her assistance. Myungsoon's goal of improving her conversational skills in English fit well with Marcia's teaching experience.

As a young mother, Myungsoon hoped to understand better what a doctor told her and comprehend her children's teachers at required parent-teacher conferences. Also, as a Catholic, she desired to worship more adequately by understanding the sermons presented in English. Furthermore, she wished to help her children with their homework. Her final aim was to possess sufficient English skills to land a part-time job.

When Marcia's student started the program, she could read notes on school papers and was acquainted with English grammar. However, Myungsoon needed pronunciation help and assistance in speaking and writing. She complained about being uncomfortable when speaking English, especially with her kids' teachers and even with her neighbors. Her interests included playing tennis, viewing movies, and playing with her children.

The difficulty in speaking and feeling comfortable using the language centered on her lack of English speaking contacts since most of her friends were Korean. Marcia encouraged her to socialize outside her Korean peer group, but this proved very hard for Myungsoon. So, her English practice was very limited. This continued to be the case the entire tutoring year. This young mother worked efficiently in class and always finished her homework on time, which Marcia appreciated. However, she would not risk or could not make the effort to venture out of her comfort zone to practice her English skill. This was a constant disappointment for Marcia.

Spending about 2¼ hours in preparation for every hour of tutoring the first two or three weeks into the program meant that Marcia was donating a lot of attention to just one student. In previous teaching, she had spent less preparation on a full day in the classroom and received pay for it. Plus, Myungsoon's two-week vacation in August interrupted the learning process. That did not make Marcia "a happy camper." But she was determined to help her student succeed.

The program required Marcia to keep detailed records of her student's progress and extensive lesson plans. These papers were submitted every couple of weeks to the program director. Apparently, Marcia's work proved acceptable since she seldom if ever received any negative feedback.

Marcia and Myungoon became friends. Myungoon brought a jewelry box as a present from Korea. One day after a session I was invited to meet the Korean student and her children. The son and older daughter spoke fluent English, but only the son could communicate in Korean. The daughter had been too young to learn Korean before coming to America.

In April 2012, when Marcia was diagnosed with stage four ovarian cancer, she immediately quit tutoring. The two parted paths, but Myungsoon Ma honored Marcia by attending her memorial service some 17 months later.

Marcia may have chosen to write about several other events in her life. One event might have been when she was chosen homecoming queen in high school at Plainfield High in Indiana. Another could have been her work with natives in British Columbia the summer after college graduation. Or, she could have cited the success she experienced in teaching either on the elementary or secondary level at McCurdy School in Española, N.M., for nearly two decades. Of course, she could have selected to tell about raising two sons on her husband's meager missionary salary. Possibly, Marcia could have spoken about her later work as a research editor at the Los Alamos Laboratories for 19 years. Then again, my wife may have related how she designed and supervised the construction of two additions to the family home in La Mesilla near Española. However, I think she would have considered tutoring as the event about which to write since it was her most recent venture and such a meaningful service at a later age. What better way to use her education and commitment to teaching than to help someone adapt to a new society.

A Worthy Delay
by
Alice Y. Jurkens

At about 12 years of age, my cousin came to visit us for a few days. She
was an RN at Cook County Hospital
in Chicago, and I admired her greatly.
She shared a bed with me, and she
slept without a pillow! I slept without a pillow for months thereafter. I
wanted to be just like her. Someday
I, too, would wear a white, starched
uniform.

After graduation from high
school, Mom took me to Chicago to investigate nursing schools.
Cook County Hospital seemed huge and cold, but just down the
street was Presbyterian Hospital School of Nursing (PHSN) and
just what I wanted. I qualified in every way except I was too young.
However, I would be accepted in the next class after a delay of six
months.

I wanted to accrue some spending money for school later, so I
applied for a position with the Prince Manufacturing Co. in Ster-
ling, Illinois. I had no qualifications, but I guess I looked like I could
learn. And learn I did: payrolls, payables and receivables, reconcil-
ing bank statements, invoicing. Fortunately, I was able to type to
cover correspondence needs.

The manufacturing company built the electric five-spindle multi-mixers that mixed five malted milks at the same time. Mr. Prince invented the machine to use in his Prince Castle 15 cent hamburger locations. He also used many paper cups in his business and a skilled salesman, Ray Kroc, was his supplier. Kroc liked the multi-mixer. He convinced Prince to give him exclusive marketing rights and sold them all over the country. One of his biggest clients was the McDonald brothers in California who eventually allowed Kroc the sole rights to market the McDonalds hamburger business (1954). All-in-all it was an interesting period for me as I awaited my move to Chicago for nursing school.

I entered the 1943 spring class at PHSN and was thrilled to be there. It was a wonderful experience, especially since we could assume much responsibility because of the remaining gap left in personnel after Presbyterian sent a large medical team to the South Pacific for the war effort. Everyone, in whatever way, wanted to do all they could to help the troops during WWII.

In late 1944, I had a visit from a hometown friend, a pilot in the Army Air Corps. He was tall, nice looking and had a breast of service ribbons on his officer's uniform. I had always thought he was nice, but now I was smitten. He had an extended furlough before departing for overseas. He visited his family but returned to Chicago so we could have more time together. We then decided we would spend our lives together after the war. In short time, he was on his way overseas flying a B-24 with his crew of 10 men going by way of Africa en route to England and the Eighth Air Force Bomb Group. I received a diamond ring in the mail a few weeks later. He had purchased it before leaving Chicago, and C. D. Peacock Jewelers sent an accompanying letter to inform me that it was from Lt. John Jurkens (no mistakes to be made here).

John returned in 1945 after 36 bombing missions over Europe and was awaiting orders to the South Pacific for air-sea rescue missions when the war was declared over.

We married after I graduated in 1946 and settled into civilian life, he in his chosen field of commercial art and I in nursing. The Korean War erupted in 1950, and John's reserve group was activated. He spent two more years in the Air Force. Near the end of this period, he became acquainted with a fledgling business that attracted his attention. It was the factor that changed our whole lives — automatic car washing. John always enjoyed washing and waxing his car. The industry, in its infancy, was a call to him to start his own business.

We had one child and another on the way, so my nursing had been put on the shelf except for a Band-Aid here or there. John's commercial art had taken a hiatus since he'd been in the service for the last two years. Hence, we were both ready to accept a new challenge. He could run the wash, and I could do the books at home (thanks to Mr. Prince).

Totally underfunded, we pushed forward. John found a man who agreed to build the building, but he wanted the last year's rent in advance. That greatly reduced our start-up finances. Only two companies offered car wash equipment in that era, but they sold it only as a package. We were unable to afford the whole package, so John went to his high school industrial arts teacher and persuaded him to build the car wash equipment as a class project. John could draw the plans exactly how he wanted the equipment to be built, and the students would build them. The plan worked.

We overcame many other problems, and the car wash opened in 1953 in Rock Island, Illinois. There were a few "bugs" in the operation, but overall it went fairly well.

We could not afford a cashier, and I was at home, 45 miles away, with the children. Thus, John would collect the $1.50 (cost of a car wash in 1953) at the end of the line where he was wiping down cars. He put the coins in one side pocket and the bills in the other. Once in a while he would have a break in the line and go back to the office to empty his pockets into a cigar box. At the end of the day he brought the cigar box home and dumped the contents on the table. I would count it so he could figure out how many cars he had washed that day.

Many obstacles were overcome, and the car wash was running well. So we decided to move on to Madison, Wisconsin, where he built a second car wash and then a third. By this time, of course, we had cashiers, but I was doing all the paper work and payrolls at home. By 1959 we had four car washes and four children. John was driving long distances to start new car washes, and I was working on the books after the kids went to bed. They learned to sleep as I sat downstairs running a hand cranked adding machine that made a lot of noise. Sometimes I would still be working when John was getting up early for a long distance drive to look into yet another car wash.

We realized we needed to make changes. For one, we called ourselves Avenue Car Washes but now one was being built on a Street, so we switched to Octopus Car Washes. John felt strongly that a business needed to have both an excellent lawyer and an excellent accountant. We had a part-time accountant, but we needed a full time top-notch one, and luckily we got the best. He was intelligent, honest and a great addition to the team.

We had an outstanding lawyer who was capable of guiding John through his creative ideas for acquiring operating car washes in which the owner just wanted out. Many people got into the business without realizing the amount of work involved, and John became known as the guy who could take over washes and make them profitable. For this reason he received a lot of phone calls.

John decided that if he showed the profit and loss statements to the key personnel of each car wash and offered each of them a share of the profit, they could see where they could save money and make their share of the profit larger. They could be "owners" without an investment. It was this that allowed the business to keep expanding.

We didn't start the business with the intent to provide room for

96

the children, but they wanted to be a part of it, and all came aboard. We grew to seven states, selling some occasionally and adding more. We were involved at one time or another with 30 car washes.

It has been a very successful business, and many employees have been with us for 20-40 years. Importantly, there has always been a sign in each office that alerts the manager, "If you are in here, who is taking care of the customer?"

In retrospect, eight years in nursing was a satisfying experience that I truly enjoyed. However, the delay in entering nurses training resulted in a job that taught me skills that were valuable in the future we chose. From the nursing profession to automatic car washing was a sharp detour but an exciting undertaking. Octopus Car Washes have given our family 60 years of gratification.

Second Career
by
Elsie Kather

Following graduation from Loret-
to Academy in Santa Fe, New Mexico,
I completed a two-year dental hygiene
program at the University of New
Mexico and became licensed to practice as a dental hygienist. I worked in
this capacity for several years, and it
served me well. It allowed me to provide for myself and my two sons following the divorce from my first husband. However, working in a small
area of the mouth was confining and limiting. In addition, patients
were not able to converse while my hands were in their mouths
cleaning their teeth. Interactions were significantly one-sided.

In March of 1977 Gary, the man I was dating, was in an auto-
mobile accident which rendered him a spinal cord injured quad-
riplegic. I became involved in his rehabilitation, and we married
three and a half years following that accident. It was during his rehabilitation and through interactions with others who were recov-
ering, in addition to recollections of the experiences I had when my
first husband had testicular cancer, that I began to realize I would
prefer a line of work where I could interact with people in a more
meaningful way.

This realization led to the decision to return to school. I was not sure what field to go into but began with psychology courses. Experience had shown me that not only psychological adjustment, but also social situations, cultural backgrounds, spiritual beliefs, and other aspects of one's being impacted how individuals adapted to crisis situations. I branched out to include these areas in my studies and finally settled on social work. I completed a Bachelor of Social Work degree from the College of Santa Fe and a master's degree from Highlands University. I wanted to work in medical social work, but not with spinal cord injured patients because that was "too close to home." I had done a field placement in a dialysis clinic and opted for that discipline. Thus, for the majority of my time as a social worker, I worked with kidney dialysis and transplant patients.

These patients ranged in age from childhood to the elderly, came from all walks of life and all socio-economic groups, espoused various religious beliefs and value systems, and, thereby, provided a well-rounded population with whom I was able to interact. Because kidney failure is a life-long illness, I enjoyed long-term relationships with many individuals and their families. I was able to help with their concrete needs by putting them in touch with different organizations that provided medical insurance, financial assistance, transportation, and support systems for adjustment. Counseling patients and members of their families toward the goal of understanding, acceptance, and a positive adjustment to their particular situation was an important aspect of my job.

As I reflect on my work as a medical social worker with renal patients, one client comes to mind as perhaps the most poignant of my encounters. Nora was 5 years old when her kidneys failed. She began hemodialysis therapy that required that she come to the clinic three times a week for a treatment that lasted about three hours each session. She was, understandably, frightened when she began. She was occasionally in tears, often shaking and reluctant to be dialyzed. I made it a point of seeing Nora each time she came for dialysis. She gradually became more comfortable and less fearful in the clinic. She greeted and talked with other patients and staff members. She even joked at times.

Nora and her family lived in a small community outside of Los Lunas and Belen. I made several home visits to assist the family in applying for End Stage Renal Disease Medicare and Medicaid to pay for treatment, to help arrange transportation to and from the clinic, and to meet with teachers and counselors at school to determine the best way to meet this child's educational goals. I started educating all involved about Nora's illness and its treatment options, and began the counseling process toward the goal of achieving a positive adjustment for all.

The family did not have the resources to do treatment at home, so peritoneal dialysis was not an option for Nora. However, kidney transplantation was an option. The family decided to complete the medical work-up and Nora was placed on the waiting list. After a period of time, she was called and received a kidney transplant. This organ worked well for Nora for about a year and a half, but then her body rejected the kidney, and she needed to return to hemodialysis. She attempted one more transplant which also failed. She and her family exhibited a great deal of resilience as they coped with one medical crisis after another. Eventually, Nora's medical condition deteriorated to the point where she was spending more time in the hospital than she was at home.

One day while I was meeting with Nora as she was receiving treatment, she asked, "What is heaven like?" I responded that I did not know, but asked what she thought heaven was like. She went on to explain that she thought heaven would be a pink house with flowers in all the windows and all around the yard. Then she talked about how, if she didn't have dialysis any more, she would die as she had witnessed through the years with other patients. I confirmed that for her. This began several months of intense conversations about death and dying with her and with members of her family, which included a grandmother who also received dialysis in our clinic and a sister who was nearing end stage renal disease. The biggest obstacle for Nora was that she could not take her mom with her to heaven. I held several counseling sessions with her and her mother regarding this issue. Nora was now 11 years old and obviously could not legally decide to stop dialysis. Her parents would need to decide and what a difficult decision that would be. Eventually, the family was ready to proceed with Nora's wishes to stop treatment and, thus, the dying process began.

I was able to continue interactions with all involved. One night, in the middle of the night, the family called me stating the hospital doctors felt that death was near. I was able to get to the University of New Mexico Hospital to be present when Nora took her last breath. I also was able to continue counseling regarding the grieving process with various members of her family. I hope that Nora is living in a pink house with flowers in all the windows and around the yard.

Nora's story epitomizes the all-encompassing interactions which I experienced in my work with kidney dialysis and transplant clients and their families. This discipline is what I chose for most of my social work career. I spent the last few years of my career working in hospice — first as a volunteer and then as a social worker. Interaction with individuals and families from a wide range of the population, once again provided me with opportunities to learn and grow, which contributed to a strong feeling of fulfillment.

Gary's paralysis was the turning point in my life that afforded me the chance to change my line of work to one which was more meaningful and rewarding. It provided me with a myriad of experiences and encounters that impacted and helped form me into the woman I am today. I am grateful to him for that opportunity and for the support he gave me through the transition, during my working years, and on-going as we share our retirement together.

French to the Rescue
by
Joyce King

After I entered the Foreign Service in 1959, I soon realized that women were regarded as less able or less valuable than their male counterparts as evidenced by rank and salary. Only men were automatically designated as officers if they passed the Foreign Service exam. Women were not given the exam but were required to type and take shorthand. They were classified as secretaries — the traditional  configuration of business offices. This assignment of women to clerical roles was the standard scenario for women entering any international government agency — including the Foreign Service, the Central Intelligence Agency (CIA), the Agency for International Development (AID), or the United States Information Service (USIS).

Many women thought that this ranking system was acceptable, partly because disparity was such a commonly accepted practice, and there had been little influence yet from the Women's Liberation Movement. Others were unhappy to take the title of secretary after having held positions of greater standing.

In my case, I had completed a master's degree in French Language and Literature and had begun work on a doctorate with plans for university teaching that I had already started. But at this juncture I had become fascinated with a sense of urgency to get to the new emerging continent of Africa — the only continent that would develop in my lifetime! I felt I had to know it before I reached the "late" age of 30. I was 29 and so eager to attain this objective that I was willing to abandon or postpone what had been a difficult academic journey. I would have to accept a demotion in career status gracefully.

My consuming passion had always been studying new languages and cultures and getting to less known exotic places where only famous adventurers had traveled and lived. So I researched the possibilities for travel and work in Africa. With no family financial backing, I had worked my way through college without incurring the usual student debt. I broke up college years with jobs on Capitol Hill where I learned about surplus food and in New York with the American Association of the United Nations which supported programs of the United Nations. During that time I also had the opportunity to work with Eleanor Roosevelt and to learn about the new nations and leaders of Africa. I checked out the different assignments for which I might qualify to serve in Africa including the military, the Peace Corps, and teaching English as a second language. Finally upon the advice of a wise mentor, I opted for the Foreign Service.

My mentor also urged me to give up flirting with a myriad of world languages and focus on thoroughly learning French in both oral and written forms. This language had been central to my academic work. I did so with the help of an excellent French professor who helped me to obtain a French Government scholarship to support a summer school immersion course. My language professor was also a master of syntax and inspired my efforts. I worked hard and spent a summer in France managing to speak and write acceptable French.

When the Foreign Service accepted me, I was not, of course, free to choose my job in my first (or any) foreign assignment. However, I had accurately placed my bet that it would be in Africa where the largest percentages of new posts were open. My assignment was in Tunis. While Tunis was not in deepest, darkest Africa (sub-Saharan Africa), it was in North Africa, and I could practice French and continue to study Arabic.

The happier development was that my French was desperately needed, and I foresaw that my days as a secretary might be numbered. The Education Division was sponsoring an international conference which they were told at the last minute had to be in French. No one had inquired about staff language qualifications, in fact, could not specify the proficiency needed to run a conference. The Director in charge was delighted to learn of my arrival and my abilities in French. I accepted the unexpected role as assistant conference administrator with delight. I have not been received with such joy nor given such accolades of appreciation since that time. Especially I was grateful since I had distant visions of a changed rank in the Foreign Service. I cared less about the rank and much more about the work I would be doing.

Tunisia was a new post and Washington lacked experience in deciding the level of French required for specific jobs. They had not yet learned how to find and hire French speakers (Canadians, Louisianans, native speakers in related professions). Many French teachers had been hired to teach French to the numerous Foreign Service community members who typically did not possess language aptitude or basics. Many had studied several years, but most had not had teachers who spoke French well. They had spent most class time on repetition of verb conjugations. Language labs were still scarce, and there were few exchange programs or emphasis on student travel abroad. Finally, most Americans believed (and still do) that they were not endowed with language facility. The French teachers did not speak English (though most, when interviewed, had said they did). Even though the State Department had made available excellent teaching materials, the young teachers (Tunisian or French) needed counsel and supervision beyond the exchanges they had with their students. I coined these teacher-student exchanges as dialogues *entre sounds* (conversations between the deaf).

The language leader in our office was leaving for a new post where her husband had taken a job, and I was asked to take her position. My unappreciated career as a secretary ended, though I retained the title and salary. It took the government months to obtain a waiver for such bold action and to make the personnel change official and with appropriate pay.

Ability to carry out jobs as they arose was useful in my next post in neighboring Algeria. Though still classified as a secretary and though the officers (of Belgian, Swiss and Canadian origin) in Algiers spoke French, we were now involved with surplus food. French was still important for converting units of food from long tons to metric tons, pounds to kilograms, hard wheat and bulgur wheat to couscous or semolina. I became a Food for Peace Officer who translated diplomatic notes for the Ambassador. Algeria, like Tunisia, had just fought a war for independence from the mother country, France, and the wheat fields in these former bread basket countries had been destroyed. People were facing hunger. Food was our major tool in the Cold War.

I spent the next 30 years as a researcher in French-speaking Africa with periodic sojourns in South America, Romania, and Egypt for AID and the World Bank. My research mainly involved weighing and measuring young children and interviewing mothers.

I was an adaptive officer, but nothing mattered more in my Foreign Service work than a thorough knowledge of French whether to train teachers, to make things work in another culture, or to enrich my environment. I never needed the doctorate or to study a lesser known 16th-century French poet. I had taken the right road.

I am happy to observe that the Foreign Service has changed

mightily for women. Today you may pick up an issue of the State Department magazine and see smiling faces of newly appointed women ambassadors and read about women being treated fairly and equally in what once was a tradition-bound Department.

The Two "Memorable Men" in My Life
by
Mary M. Kinney

The first "memorable man" was my father. He was the youngest of 10, born on a farm in southern Wisconsin. His parents were Irish Catholic and very devoted to their faith. He married my mother and had two daughters. After five years of marriage, my mother passed away after falling on the ice and hitting her head. I was 4 years old and my sister Peggy was almost 2. Dad had help from rela-  tives sometimes, but he was the main parent. We spent a lot of time with our mother's relatives. They were so good to us. When I was 10 years old and Peggy was 8, it was just the three of us living on the same farm where Dad was born.

We learned to do everything. Dad took us with him everywhere. Shirley Temple was popular at this time. He took us to all of her movies. I think the cost of the movies at that time was 11 cents. We always went to church on Sundays. He was a "fun-loving" person who enjoyed singing and dancing. I learned to play the piano, so we sang a lot. He taught us the words to so many songs.

We all took turns cooking, and we ate lots of chicken, since Dad raised them. I remember one time he used a pressure cooker, and the pressure regulator flew off! The kitchen was covered with chicken. So Dad decided to hire the "town drunk," Jigs, to wallpaper the kitchen walls. In exchange for wallpapering, Dad bought him some beer. Well, he must have been drunk while wallpapering, because when he finished we saw that the flowers were upside down. Rather than take it down, we just left it up. As we always said, "That was good enough!"

Dad made sure we always went to school. He would see what other girls our age were wearing and take us shopping so we would be in style. He also would take us to get our hair fixed. At that time permanents were in style. I remember being hooked up to this machine, and by the time we were done our hair was "very frizzy." We could hardly get a comb or brush through it.

Dad influenced my life by the way he lived his. Religion was very important to him as it is to me now. He always took care of Peggy and me. He never left us alone. He taught us to live by the Golden Rule: "Do unto others as you would have them do unto you." I have taught my children to live by this rule.

We both left the farm after high school and moved to Madison, Wisconsin. Dad married again, but not until we girls were on our own. He developed Parkinson's disease in his 60s, and he died at age 76. I will always remember that Dad was a very kind and wonderful man.

The second "memorable man" in my life was my husband, Bob. He was also born into a large Irish Catholic family in South Dakota. He spent a couple of years in the Navy and later graduated from Creighton University in Omaha, Nebraska.

Dad always wanted me to marry an Irish Catholic, so he was very happy with Bob. We met and married in Denver, Colorado. Our four children were all born in Denver. We had one son and three girls: Kevin, Anne, Joan and Nancy. Bob worked as an insurance adjuster for many years and the last 20 years of his life he worked for the federal government. He was dependable, loved to cook, and was very handy around the house.

We were transferred to Minneapolis, Minnesota, in 1967. Apple Valley was a suburb where we lived for 17 years. It was like "Suburbia USA." All the streets were named after apples, and everyone had an apple tree in their backyard. All the neighbors would get together and help each other. Bob had many friends and socialized with them often. There were 50 children on our street and the women stayed home and took care of their kids. We had a "Tom and Jerry" Christmas Party every year. All the neighbors would come to have Bob's "Tom and Jerrys," a warm eggnog drink very popular in the Midwest. Bob's dad also made them every Christmas Eve. Apple Valley almost sounds like Lake Wobegon!! As Garrison Keillor said, "… where the women are strong, the men are all handsome and the children are above average."

There were eight children in Bob's family, and when his mother died she had over 50 grandchildren. Most of his siblings had large families. Every three years the Kinneys have a family reunion. Between 150 to 200 people attend. We have had the reunions in many places, including Denver, San Diego, Chicago, Albuquerque, Sioux Falls, Rapid City, and Spokane. The reunions are held on a weekend. On Saturday evening we have a dinner/dance with a video slideshow. On Sunday we enjoy a picnic with the whole family. Needless to say, everyone has a good time and enjoys visiting with all the relatives. Bob and I attended all of the reunions.

Bob's job transferred us to Albuquerque, New Mexico, in 1984. It was difficult to leave Apple Valley and all our friends. It took a while to adjust to New Mexico because it was a desert and so different from Apple Valley. But as time went on we did adjust and now we all like Albuquerque very much. We especially like the weather. Bob got tired of the Minnesota winters, with shoveling snow and our cars not working. We did not miss the snow, although our kids loved it there and always talked about the good childhood they had in Minnesota.

Bob and I always wanted to go to Ireland, and we finally went in 1995. We went on a bus tour with a tour guide. The tour included many places where our ancestors were born. It was a very enjoyable, fun trip with many other Irish people. We also went on several cruises. The first one was to the Caribbean. We also cruised to Alaska and Hawaii. Our favorite cruise line was Holland America Line. Bob had many relatives in Vista, California. We visited them several times during the years.

Bob was a wonderful family man. He was very supportive of all of us. He always worked to give us a good life. He had a good sense of humor and made us all laugh often.

Bob worked until he was 70 years old. In March of 2006 he went to the hospital for elective surgery, which was not supposed to be serious. Complications set in, and he passed away on April 1, 2006. He had just turned 81 in March 2006.

Bob and I always prayed together. We attended Mass every Sunday. I think of him often and feel blessed that I had a good marriage for 47 years.

A Still, Small Voice
by
Lorraine Mae Kunsman

My dad worked for the Atchison, Topeka and Santa Fe Railway and as a child we moved from town to town, wherever the railroad sent us. The railroad company provided housing for its employees. I can remember many of the Colorado and New Mexico towns where we lived. Some of those towns no longer exist. When it was time for me to go to school, my folks moved back to settle down in Trinidad, Colorado.

After I graduated from Trinidad High School, in 1944, my mother took me to La Junta, Colorado, to apply for a job at the *El Otero*, a Harvey House restaurant. At that time there were few decent employment options for young girls. A Harvey House was considered a good place to work for girls my age because the reputation of a *Harvey Girl* was much respected. Fred Harvey set many requirements that guided the behavior of the *Harvey Girls*.

However, not all of the restaurant managers observed all of Fred Harvey's requirements. One requirement was to sign a six-month contract stipulating that the new hire work for the full six months, follow rules and regulations of conduct and behavior, and

113

not get married. As it turned out, it was fortunate that I wasn't given a contract to sign when the manager hired me.

We had more training and benefits than some other jobs for young women at that time. Meals and rooms for the girls were provided. The salary was about $17.50 per month, but we could keep all of our tips. The waitress uniform of white shirt, small black tie, wraparound white skirt and white starched apron was provided along with laundry service. I was glad I didn't have to wear the long black skirt that former waitresses had to wear. We were expected to be neat and tidy at all times and conduct ourselves as *ladies*.

Other rules applied to the conduct of customers in the restaurant. Young men were expected to behave like gentlemen, and the waitresses were not supposed to flirt with them. However, there was one nice young man, named Bill, who I *sneaked* out to date a few times.

I was taught how to greet customers, be polite, take orders, and finally, with some difficulty, balance three hot plates of food or beverage on one arm. I learned quickly and could soon write up the bills, work at the cash register, clear tables and set up the clean place settings for new customers. I liked working there very much, and I liked the other girls — we had a good time.

I was never sure why, but one day, the head-waitress decided that on Monday nights, only one waitress was needed. She appointed me, and that meant that I had to wait table, clear it, act as cashier and reset the table — all by myself. That was a lot of work for one person. I did it one night and wasn't happy with that situation.

I'd met and waited on a lot of nice people who came into the restaurant, especially two regular ones who had been telling me of another job with the railroad. I talked to them a little bit more about that railroad job. When I had some time off, I went to the railroad office and applied for that job, which was called a *messenger* who hand-delivered messages throughout the office. They hired me but told me I had to be released from Harvey House.

114

Well, I knew the manager could not make me stay because I had not signed anything. I went to the State Employment Agency, and they gave me a statement releasing me from the restaurant. When I told the manager I was quitting, he was mad. He said, "Get your stuff and get out — *now!*" I did as I was told.

I took the train back to Trinidad because I had to get a signature from my mother. Mother's mother, my grandmother, didn't want me to quit working for the Harvey House, but Mother understood and thought it was all right. She signed the *Minor's Release* form, and I went to Las Vegas, New Mexico, to train as an *apprentice PBX operator* for the Atchison, Topeka and Santa Fe Railway.

My high school yearbook had described me as "*A small, still voice.*" But I had been brought up to know right from wrong and that life took courage, honesty and adaptability. Sometimes I had to change my mind and decide what to do that was right for me.

Taking that job with the railroad was the important turning point in my life. I was lucky. The Harvey House where I worked closed in 1958, but the trains still ran. I stayed with the railroad, learned how to do new things and moved upward to better positions until I retired in 1985. I never regretted my decision to leave Harvey House and work for the railroad. It provided me with a good career and good benefits as a retiree. I always felt my dad would have liked knowing that I followed in his footsteps — working for the railroad.

And now I see that being a Harvey Girl, even for that short time, placed me in a little bit of the history of the Southwest. I have enjoyed that. However, moving on to work for the Atchison, Topeka and Santa Fe Railway gave me more opportunities and a career.

Never Too Late
by
Jane Lovato

"You are never too old to set another goal or to dream a new dream." — C. S. Lewis

"I'll never be able to paint in watercolor! Let's go home." Those were the words I exclaimed to my husband after taking my first class in watercolor at the Tucson Museum of Art. My husband Henry Lovato smiled. That week he bought some brushes, paints and paper and declared, "We are going to class." He did, and we did, for several weeks, until I could mix color and not always get "mud." By now, you can surmise that my husband was a very strong man; he had survived the Bataan Death March and imprisonment by the Japanese. And now, I was so very fortunate to have him and his support.

Before I married Henry, I had a conversation with the elegant and extraordinary "Concha" Ortiz y Pino de Kleven, who, at the time, was serving on the board of the Lovelace Clinic in Albuquerque, New Mexico. I told her that I was to be married and the next time she stopped by my office at Lovelace Clinic, my name would be Jane Lovato. Maria Concepción "Concha" Ortiz y Pino de Kleven told me that when I married a Hispanic man, I would become his property, as signified by the proper change of my name to *Jane de Lovato*. I liked the rhythm of the name and remembered it. I knew she was hinting at the world of culture I was about to enter.

After I had retired from Lovelace Clinic at age 62, I went to school to become a professional fashion model. I loved clothes, and in this way I could wear beautiful garments without buying them. Modeling gigs were enjoyable and personally rewarding because I was involved in the business of style, beauty, coordination and presentation.

My creative urges were stimulated, and I decided I would like to try painting. I discussed this with Henry, and that is when he suggested I enroll in the class at the Museum. For several weeks, Henry went with me and became a steadfast support person in my life. I cannot imagine my life without painting: the joy of color, the excitement of development, and the ultimate framing of an idea.

Beginning to paint was certainly a turning point in my life. My new life as an artist was always amazing. The artists I met became soul mates.

To exhibit art in Santa Fe, New Mexico, seemed like the ultimate; I decided to peddle my paintings to galleries or any well-trafficked businesses. So, with a kitchen potholder wrapped around the hanging wires of my paintings in order to protect my hand, I carried my wares door-to-door in Santa Fe. I encountered many refusals, but eventually my signature chile paintings were hung in a most reputable culinary business — The Cookworks. I enjoyed many trips to Santa Fe to check on my sales and always had a good time.

I was very fortunate to be accepted in local, state and national shows. I exhibited in a lovely gallery in Tubac, Arizona. Also, I was so proud to have been in the Survivors of Cancer traveling art shows, which included an exhibition at the Roundhouse in Santa Fe. The Creede Repertory Theatre in Creede, Colorado, honored me when they selected my painting of Creede to be the "poster of the year" for their Centennial Celebration. We printed 500 posters, and to my knowledge, they were all sold or given as gifts. Other places my artwork was shown were country clubs, restaurants, business locations, and the Albuquerque Parade of Homes open houses. From the latter I received many commissions that enabled me to "fill my sugar bowl." For several years, I was the curator of artwork at El Pinto Restaurant in Albuquerque. During that time, I sold many paintings, including one to the Director of Animation at Walt Disney Studios. He purchased it as a gift for his wife.

One of my successful ventures involved chiles. I attended a workshop that inspired me to paint chiles. In order to have a model, I went to where they were roasting chiles, picked up some rejects from the ground, took these home, scrubbed them, and began my career in chile paintings. These paintings became my trademark. I once had an Asian man buy one, telling me he was taking it to Alaska. To my great delight my chile paintings hang in many kitchens, libraries, offices, and dining rooms. It is a wonder and a thrill to know that I have paintings in France, in England, in Scotland, all over the United States, and who knows where else. What a life!

My dear husband did all my framing. He was my mat cutter and hung many shows for me. Henry was also tolerant of my attempt at panache when I remembered what Maria Concepción "Concha" Ortiz y Pino de Kleven had said to me and chose a *nom de guerre*, or, in my case, a *nom de brush*, signing my paintings "Jane de Lovato." When we received mail addressed to Henry de Lovato, he just smiled. This story is a tribute to him, for I would never have painted if he hadn't bought supplies, attended classes with me and encouraged me.

By this time, you can see why I called this story "Never Too Late." For, at age 65, I picked up brushes and met a challenge. Watercolor was to become a great new chapter in my life. Thank you, Henry, for making me an artist.

The Honeymoon Trunk
by
Ann Lewis Lovekin

"Pardon me, Ma'am. I would rec-
ognize Helen Hayes anywhere! Will
you please give me your autograph?"
Many times in public places — trains,
airplanes, museums, or just walking
down the street in Washington —
Mother would hear similar words to
these. With her silver hair piled high,
a dark ribbon of grey hair traversing
the top of her head, and an elegant
comb placed at just the right angle,
Mildred McNeill Lewis would turn heads in almost any situation.
Her smiling, sky blue eyes, erect, confident posture with head held
high or tilted back in laughter, gave her a friendly air of approach-
ableness. She was born in 1890 in South Carolina and reared in
Southern gentility, the second of four living children. She looked
much like her father, a tall, redheaded blue-eyed Scotsman.

Mother fell in love at first meeting with my father, a Virginia
Lewis from Albemarle County. He was a civil engineer and worked
for the State of South Carolina. They soon married and had a three-
week honeymoon in New Orleans. In 1922, my brother William
Strayer Lewis, Jr. was born in Florence, S.C. The little family moved
from one challenging job to another up and down the Eastern sea-

121

board but always south of the Mason-Dixon Line as promised to Mother!

The Roaring Twenties were just that and the Florida Boom was good to them. However, the Florida Bust came in 1927, and Daddy and Uncle Meriwether, his younger brother, were forced to close the Lewis Engineering firm in St. Petersburg. "Bro" and Aunt Mary came back to his Virginia parents as did Mother and Daddy and little Billy, only theirs was a more circuitous route involving several jobs and moves. Mother always packed her honeymoon trunk with silver, china, linens and pictures to make "home" at the next place.

The Great Depression was in full swing in 1931 when I was born as a surprise! Mother was 41 by then. Early on I knew that my role in the family was to be "Little Miss Sunshine." It came easily to me as Mother was naturally optimistic and good-natured and a woman of deep faith in God, in His love and goodness and providence. She loved the Episcopal liturgy, and I have loved it also. I actually have spent many of my happiest times in the sacristy doing altar work as Mother did. We sang the Canticles together as we washed and polished. At home, she was busy embroidering crosses and rolling hems on the altar linens, and mending those that needed it. She did altar work for over 80 years until her death at age 95. I have had the wonderful privilege of serving for over 60 years, due mostly to her influence.

We moved to Maryland, Washington, D.C., Norfolk, Virginia, and then back to Maryland. The honeymoon trunk made every place a home very quickly, and Mother's attitude about it all — her excitement and anticipation at the thought of new adventures and challenges — was contagious. Always, the first Sunday after arriving in a new place, we went to church and met the Rector and families who would become our faith community.

There were so many old sayings that peppered Mother's conversations, i.e., "Water seeks its own level" (re: friends); "Remember who you are"; "Lift others up"; "Consider the other's point of view";

"Think before you speak"; "Always be gracious"; "You are a Southern Lady." "Feed the hungry and visit the sick" was a sort of mantra
to Mother. It seemed to us that we were always preparing food for
neighbors and strangers in need. Bill, as a child, remembers helping
her pick apples, pack them into boxes and bags, and put them out
on the roadside for anyone to take. I remember helping her pack
lunch boxes for hungry ones who came to our door.

Family and friends near and far were especially dear to Mother,
and it was important to keep in touch. Aunt Sue wrote faithfully
every Sunday beginning with "Dearest Sit" (Sister) and Mother responded every Tuesday. She and I wrote weekly for many decades.
I still have her letters.

I'll always remember the two years we lived in Washington,
D.C. I was 8 and 9 then. Daddy worked for the federal government. However, his heart health was precarious, and he had many
hospitalizations. Times were very hard for us, and the honeymoon
trunk made home in three different furnished apartments. Mother
stopped driving then, and so we walked or took the city bus. Bill
took a job with the U.S. Postal Service and rode his bicycle around
the city delivering telegrams. I recall him wearing a blue uniform
that was just the color of his eyes. I thought him to be so handsome. Somehow, Mother saw to it that we took every advantage to
go and see and do while living in our nation's Capital. During days
at home, she made almost all of my clothes and hers. Fashion was
always important to her, so she either designed or copied beautiful
outfits and hats.

We belonged to St. John's, Lafayette Square, known as the
"Presidents' church." Sometimes we worshipped at the Cathedral of
St. Peter and St. Paul — the National Cathedral. (Only Bethlehem
Chapel in the undercroft was open for services then.) Our cousin,
Hunter Lewis, was Rector of Epiphany in downtown Washington,
and we went there often for noonday services.

We frequently visited the White House (and went to the Easter

Egg rolls), the Capitol, the Library of Congress, the Lincoln Memorial. We toured the old red brick Smithsonian Institution where Charles Lindbergh's plane, "The Spirit of St. Louis," hung in the entrance, and the elegant inaugural ball gowns of the presidents' wives were displayed. The Washington Monument was one of our favorites. If the elevator line was long, and he could get a head start, Bill would run up the 532 steps and try to beat us to the top!

The honeymoon trunk accompanied us to Norfolk, Va., where Daddy began work for the Navy. Now he was much stronger. It was a happy move for Mother. At last we could take our furniture out of storage and feel a sense of permanence. Many Lewis relations were fairly close by in Charlottesville and Uncle Meriwether and Aunt Mary were just a ferryboat ride away in Newport News.

After Pearl Harbor was attacked, Bill volunteered for the paratroopers and was assigned to the 82nd Airborne Division. He was wounded in Europe and awarded the Purple Heart. We went to the theatre every time the newsreels changed. We never stayed for the movie but would come back home and listen to Lowell Thomas on the radio. Mother squared her shoulders and put on a brave face, as did all the Blue Star and Gold Star mothers and wives. She jumped into the war effort by rolling bandages, sending CARE packages, knitting sox and scarves, and dealing with rationing. She wrote Bill every day. Daddy was a Block Captain during the blackouts up and down the coast. We all knew that not a single flicker of light could show at night.

The honeymoon trunk travelled with us to Southern Maryland when I was 12. The new Naval Air Test Center was being laid out on thousands of acres of rich farmland and waterfront property. Daddy was employed by the Navy to build the infrastructure for the town that was to grow up outside of the base. Mother set about helping to establish this new community "in the middle of nowhere," as she described it. She helped start a community church with a Methodist pastor. She was instrumental in establishing an Episcopal mission. She helped start a Homemakers Club and a Girl Scout troop.

My father died suddenly of a heart attack when in his 50s. I was 18 and away at a girls' school. His death was a terrible shock and a terrible loss. Subsequently, Mother and Bill encouraged me to work and save until I could attend the University of Maryland at College Park. Bill married and Mother went to live with Aunt Sue and Uncle Henley in North Carolina.

Following graduation with a Bachelor of Arts degree, I was employed by the Diocese of Washington as a Woman College Worker. Mother came to live with me that year. Then I married an Air Force 2nd Lt. whom I had met in college.

Our marriage lasted 17 years, eight of which we lived overseas. We constantly moved in the Air Force. Mother visited for a month every year wherever we were stationed, except for Guam, which she could not visit. I had my first two babies there. As a grandmother and a great-grandmother now, I can only imagine how painful it was for Mother to be separated from her daughter at that time. She never heard my voice in two years and letters took three weeks roundtrip.

I had five children in seven and a half years in three countries. However, memories of the honeymoon trunk and the lessons I had learned from Mother about how to make a home ANYWHERE, and then look forward to new challenges and adventures, gave me a "Can Do" attitude that carried us through the hard times as well as the good.

One year Mother booked passage on the Queen Mary to come and see us all. She loved and truly enjoyed her 10 grandchildren, for Bill had five also. She used our home in Germany as the starting point and resting point for 10 months of touring in Europe. She made friends wherever she went and corresponded with many of her travel companions for years.

Due to the loving care of my brother Bill, Mother lived in her own home near Bill and his family for the rest of her life. In those later years, she enjoyed everything to do with her church and the Altar Guild, doing fine sewing and smocking, making her famous three-day orange marmalade for family and friends, and entertaining her bridge clubs. She read the entire Washington Post every morning with two cups of coffee and went to bed at night with a glass of cool sherry. She could quote the sports stats like a pro, a skill she said she learned from Uncle Henley. She walked one to two miles every day until well into her 90s. (In inclement weather she would climb stairs.) Her front door stayed unlocked, except at night, so a stream of friends visited all day every day and Mother loved it.

Over the years, Mother came to appreciate Albuquerque and the unique light and art of New Mexico. We saw the first Hot Air Balloon Fiesta together. She came as often as possible in subsequent Octobers just to take in the beauty and excitement of the Fiesta with her family.

I am so blessed to be her daughter, and my children are blessed to have known and been loved by their exceptional grandmother.

"I can. I will. No doubts!" "Not dumb. Forward thinking. No limits."
by
Martha K. Mann

As a young child I was always made to feel dumb. I grew up left-handed and could not use scissors; I could not use a ladle or a serrated knife; I read and wrote backwards. The family tried to encourage me to use my right hand, but that only made me more confused and angry. The kids at school made matters worse by teasing me. The teachers tried to teach me to read by putting me on a "reading machine" which made life harder because I was not allowed to go outside with my friends, but had to sit beside the principal for the time they were at recess. I was not a happy camper.

I learned very fast that I had to find a way to think for myself, learn things I wanted to learn. I became quite rebellious at people always telling me, "You are dumb and stupid!" I am NOT either of these two labels. I learned very fast that I thought outside the box. I was not stupid — I just thought differently. I do believe the adults were trying to help, but did not understand the problem that today is called *dyslexia*. As time went on I learned wonderful things: cartography, geography, plants and animals. I loved science and art.

In the fifth grade I was made to change to a public school to see if that would help, but this was not effective and I returned to the private school. I was made to repeat a year, which infuriated me. I made the decision then that I would fight to do my very best — no matter how long it took me to achieve the goal. The project or whatever I did was going to be done well.

Throughout these early years my grandmother (we called her "Bubby") was the one who took me under her wing and gave me tools to move in a positive direction. I spent weekends with her in her apartment. We learned about things together, enjoying the alphabet and all the words I could learn. We worked on our writing, which for a left-handed person was a problem. But Bubby showed me how to write with my hand not curled around the paper. We sorted through her jewelry. I combed her hair. We just spent hours together. No yelling, no negative things, just a caring and wonderful Bubby!!! She was always there to make life tolerable. She was always showing me and teaching me something. To this day she is forever in my heart. She died 51 years ago just before I met my amazing husband. I am sorry they did not meet as she would have loved him as much as I do after 48 years of marriage. Dad also encouraged me and aided when he could. He, too, was important in my life, but Bubby was the one who taught me, guided me and gave me the tools needed to have a wonderful and fulfilling career and life with my Phil.

As I got older, life at home continued to be very difficult. But I believe now everyone tried the best they could. They just did not understand I was really starting to do good things with my life, but the things were not what they wanted me to do!

At school I was mentored by a science teacher, Lillian Potter, who allowed me to continue with experiments that went far beyond what the other students did. We spent hours working on projects together during and after school. Biology and anatomy were my favorites. By then my English teacher, Barbara Stanhope, and history teacher, Elizabeth Giangreco, took me under their wings, and I grew to love Shakespeare, the classics and history. Darn hard reading but I read every word. I would read out loud to myself. And my life was slowly becoming good.

I initially went to a two-year college as I was not sure what I wanted to do. I majored in commercial art and ceramics and did some study in photography. Then I went on to Michigan State University where I would major in Art and Veterinary Science. Through all of this my parents were not happy, but I needed to find MY way. I just found so much excitement in learning and thinking through art and especially science.

I returned to Boston in 1963 where I met my husband, Phil. Bubby had passed away one month before I met Phil. We married in 1965. It was then I began working as a medical-surgical photographer at Beth Israel Hospital for seven years. I was experiencing love for the type of activities I truly enjoyed. I photographed all surgeries, especially the early days of open heart and neurosurgery. There were many positive things going on in surgery throughout my years as their photographer. At this teaching hospital, my work was exacting and important for the doctors' research, publications and especially to their patients.

My work, again, was a problem for my parents as they wanted me in another job in which their friends would approve. Working in a hospital setting exposed me to the operating rooms, morgues and patients but, in their eyes, did not provide visible status.

Then I moved into the Surgical Research Division as an Animal Technician, where I happily spent two formative years. In 1972 I was asked by a newly appointed Chief of Immunology, Dr. Stuart Schlossman, to move with him to what is now the Dana-Farber Cancer Institute in Boston. It was a great honor to be asked to join him and his Division when they moved, and I ended up spending 28 years as Director of the Animal Research Laboratories. I was so proud of this honor and until this day no one truly understands what it meant to me — to be trusted and cared about by a newly appointed Chief. I was ready and not scared. Dr. Schlossman was always there to teach and guide me throughout our years together. He was hard and demanding, but that is what I needed. He had very high expectations and goals for all the people who worked with him.

As Director, I was responsible for creating a division of research that became the gold standard of animal research throughout the United States. In addition, I was tasked to redesign and update the animal facility with the goal of the Division being accredited. Again in 1982, 1988 and 1992, I was challenged to design three more vivarium — each one adding the latest state-of-the-art equipment and air handling. In addition, each new design increased the size of the units to allow for expanding research. The designs consistently improved our control of the cleanliness in the unit to assure the safety of the animals and the researchers and developed unique containment units which allowed for research using high-risk factors.

The most important work I did as Director was to assure the competent and compassionate care of all the animals in our facilities. Our highly competent staff, trained and supervised by myself and others, utilized "best practice" techniques that assured the comfort, well-being and health of the animals. For many years, the National Institutes of Health identified our practices as the prototype and model for others to attain, and numerous other research facilities learned and utilized our practices and procedures. The Institute remains very proud of the translational research that has been achieved — from bench to bedside!

Even though I was the Director, I was always with the animals. I didn't care if it was holding a little mouse that needed a bit of extra caring or sleeping next to a dog that had been through surgery. I was referred to as "Mother Mouse" even though we cared for many kinds of animals. Compassionate care is the bottom line — making sure that every animal is cared for lovingly and kindly.

I have often been told that my caring for, nurturing and protecting the animals created the milieu that led to ongoing success of the research being conducted. I believe the animals knew that I would never let anyone harm or hurt them. Our motto at the Animal Research Laboratories became "We care for and we love all animals that are brought in under our care."

The lady responsible, Bubby, gave me the ability to see positively and guided me in positive directions that I have carried throughout my life and career. Her willingness to let me express myself, even though differently from others, set the stage for how and what I have been able to achieve: compassion and giving back where and when I can. There was a toughness that Bubby showed me — hard work and exactness. I love all animals, and I can only thank Bubby for teaching me how to care.

A side note: The President of the Dana-Farber Cancer Institute, Dr. Baruj Benacerraf, who trusted and guided me, was also dyslexic!!! He gave me tools for how to handle many situations. Dr. Benacerraf always said, "Dyslexia is a challenge to overcome rather than a deficiency to be sorry about. To achieve excellence, I found that I always needed to examine my work with a merciless critical eye. It is far better to be more severe and demanding of oneself than others can be."

Having a Wonderful Family
by
Marina de Vos Mauney

My parents, Izaak and Cornelia de Vos, were married in the Netherlands in the city of Rotterdam, shortly before World War II. They moved to a little town just outside of Rotterdam after they married. They loved each other very much. Under difficult circumstances and during the best of times, my parents provided protection, love and good times for our family.

They had my brother Dirk-Cornelis in 1942, and I was born in the winter of 1944 during the middle of the war. It was a very cold winter, and there were no doctors available at the time. Food was scarce, times were hard, and there were bombing raids every night. My father got on his bike (that had no tires) each night to see if there were any farmers who would sell him a little rice for his baby girl. My mother was unable to nurse me, and there was no milk that I could drink. He told me that farmers always had some food for babies.

The war ended in May of 1945, and life became a little better. In 1948 my parents again became parents to my younger brother Jan. It was wonderful for all of us to have a new baby in peace time.

For two weeks in the summer months, my parents rented living space on a chicken farm in Rockanje on the beach in the south of the Netherlands. We did this for 20 years. This farm was a free range chicken farm with 5,000 chickens. It was wonderful — a childhood highlight provided by my parents.

Every day we were allowed to feed the chickens and gather the eggs. All the chickens ran loose in the fields. We could have one egg each morning — much different than at home where we could have one egg a week on Sunday only. The chicken farm had pear and plum orchards, and glass greenhouses filled with wonderful tomatoes and green beans on poles. We were able to pick them each day. At the time I did not appreciate how wonderful fresh fruit and vegetables were right out of the fields. Today, when flying into the Netherlands, one sees a sea of greenhouses. Most vegetables are grown inside because of unreliable weather conditions.

For the first few years that we were at the farm for our summer vacation, the farmhouse had no water or toilet facilities. It had a well that was outside. To get water for the house, you needed to lower a bucket on a rope and haul it up full of water. We kids loved to do that. As time went on, the chicken farm became more modern with hot and cold running water, a shower and a toilet — all inside.

It also had a *"bed stee,"* a bed placed sideways into a wall closet. It had three drawers from the floor up and the bed was above the drawers. The *bed stee* had doors on it, and you were to close the doors when you went to bed. In the old days the baby would sleep in the bottom drawer. I did not close the doors at night — that was just too scary. Remember, I was only 5 at the time. You can see a *bed stee* in Dutch paintings from the 1700s. We had such great times there.

Each morning we gathered up our beach things for the walk to the shore. We walked 5 kilometers through the beautiful dunes. On the beach, we had a rented tent for our two weeks each year, and we parked our belongings in the tent for the day. We spent the day swimming in the ocean, building sand castles, and playing ball.

Each day on our way back home from the beach to the chicken farm, again a 5 kilometer walk, we each got to choose a treat like an ice cream cone, a Mars bar or salted licorice (a big treat in the Netherlands). I always chose a Mars bar. It was all so delightful. We never got anything like that at home.

My dad, who was a marine architect, worked either in his office or at the building sites in the Netherlands or France. On our vacations he loved to fish. He would go fishing after he and my mother had their morning coffee. (Nothing can be done before they had their coffee with a cookie at ten o'clock in the morning — very Dutch.) My father fished each morning for a few hours. He never caught anything in 19 years. He wore his fishing shorts that were very big with lots of pockets. My mother thought they were the ugliest shorts ever. My father never looked very good in them, but they were his most loved shorts.

We kids were growing up. We had been going to the beach each summer for 20 years. The last summer we all were home was a special summer to go to Rockanje one more time. My father went fishing one more time also and, lo and behold, he caught an eel. What an eel it was! Huge — at least 1 meter long. He was so proud of it and showed it to my mother who thought that it was the ugliest fish ever. She ran away with her arms in the sky saying, "Please get rid of that thing." Not my father. He said, "Do not worry. I will clean and cook it. It will be our special dinner tonight — fresh fish from the ocean. You will never have had anything so good and fresh." That evening, my father cleaned the eel, sautéed it in butter, and served it with sautéed potatoes and fresh green beans. It was a feast. Even my mother liked it. Growing up in the Netherlands you have to love fish. We had herring (raw), smoked eel, oysters, mussels, *langoustine* — all right out of the ocean, fresh each day.

My parents traveled a lot due to my father's work and for pleasure. As we became older, they took us with them during the summer vacation time. We traveled all through Europe and got to see the beautiful countryside. We frequently traveled in France, since my father did a lot of work there.

During the time I was growing up and going to school in the Netherlands, we had to learn three languages besides Dutch. I never thought that was fair. Why did we have to learn all those languages? I was not going to live anywhere but in the Netherlands. However, as I got older and found out that no one speaks Dutch anywhere else but in the Netherlands, I understood why it was so important.

The Netherlands is a very small country, but it is very big in international business. The Dutch are the best at anything to do with water. They have fought against water all their lives. They still, to this day, recover land from the ocean.

Our love of the water gave us a wonderful opportunity to learn how to sail, windsurf and anything to do with water sports. My father and I were big into rowing (sculling). Whenever I see someone sculling, I think of my father. My brothers and I love sailing, and we are still doing that today.

As a young adult, I wanted to get into mechanical engineering that was not for a girl to do at that time. My parents encouraged me, and I found the confidence to do what I wanted to do. I have followed my dream into an interesting and successful work career.

I'm very grateful to have had such great parents and such a wonderful family. My parents gave us courage and a positive attitude leaving all of us with a "can do" spirit. There is no such thing as, "No. I cannot do that."

The Best of Everything
by
Peg Merrell

My life has been an ongoing educational experience. Its most influential people were my mother and
my husband, so I guess my "turning
point" was my time at Smith, when I
got away from one and met the other.

I was the last of four gifted children of gifted parents who met in an
English literature class at Washington
University in St. Louis. My mother
(27) was an academic prodigy finish-
ing her MA. Financial need had caused her to spend seven years
alternating a year of college with a year as a rural school teacher.
My father (22) was an innocent troubadour and an aspiring author.

Their first child, my sister, was pretty, bright, loving, and a delight to all the surrounding adults. However, their second child,
Billy, was born near-blind and with physical problems that preoc-
cupied his parents and doctors for nine years until he died when
my surviving brother was 7 and I was 5 years old. Shortly thereafter,
we moved to Winnetka, Illinois. I have almost no memory of Billy
or my parents during this time, but more of Andre, who took care
of cars and broken toys and carried Billy up and down stairs, and
his wife Madeleine, who was my friend and comforter.

Probably only those who have lived with a "special" child can understand how such families cope or become dysfunctional. My parents had been engrossed in Billy and were devastated by his death, but were sadly blind to the needs of their other children. My father had lost his innocence and badly damaged his lute. My mother mourned Billy for years. My sister was in high school, and later said her reaction was that maybe now they would have time for the other children. I was a detached free-wheeling comet, but my surviving brother was the most badly scarred. Many years later, my mother told me that "Tuck" had come to them after Billy died and said he was sorry it hadn't been him instead, since he knew they would rather have kept Billy. She also told me she had really wanted Tuck to be born, so that Billy would have someone to play with.

In Winnetka, we had the Best of Everything: schools, music teachers, sports equipment, a house full of books, all Chicago's cultural offerings. How do I know? My mother told us, repeatedly. The only missing items were praise, affection and humor. My father became the man who came to dinner (and then disappeared into his study), bought theater tickets, and took us to expensive restaurants, and my mother was She Who Must Be Obeyed. During the summer I spent my days at the library and the beach, and Tuck went birding. He took possession of a third-floor maid's room, out of sight of the neatness patrol, and played chess with a friend while I participated in every available sport and took up bridge. I received a lot of mixed messages: "You must think for yourself" alternated with "What will the neighbors think?"

When I was in high school, my father was developing the "invisible" brain tumor which killed him in 1945. My mother, at the time, concentrated her energies on her various civic responsibilities, but always found time to supervise my Latin. I maintained my perfect academic record, but she felt things were too easy for me. "You won't get away with this at Smith!" she warned me.

But I did get away with it. My first year at Smith was uninspiring (text, lecture, exam). I lost interest in academic achievement, but was a first-class crammer and bull artist, and I did well in courses that interested me. "Just like your father!" my mother complained. Having been her last best hope for an Ivy-style academician, I was her greatest disappointment.

In 1946 Amherst (just down the road from Smith) was inundated with returning veterans who had treasured their college memories through the war and were ready to relax and play. I met Ned Merrell that spring, and we had an idyllic college romance before getting married after graduation in 1948. After a very "gentlemanly" college record, Ned started an MBA degree at Indiana University and fell in love with widgets, therbligs, and time-and-motion. He followed me around with a stopwatch and made helpful suggestions, such as "Try washing the dishes from left to right instead of right to left." Problem-solving was in his blood and became the base of his business success: unhappy typists, warehouse accidents, branch management, corporate civil war, whatever.

We spent 36 years in St. Louis County, where my occupations included: on-site caregiver to five minor children (27 years), social studies teacher (9 years), League of Women Voters boards and committees (25+years), and real estate broker(occasional). In 1985 we moved to New Mexico, Ned's long-term goal since camping here in 1939. We had a role reversal: I got a secretarial job at the University of New Mexico's School of Management and Ned was a volunteer and tennis star. Thanks to my dedication, impeccable grammar and excellent typing, I became an Editorial Assistant. I liked working with "my" professors and participating in the introduction of computers. I enjoyed my job enough to continue several years past retirement age.

What became of these gifted people? My mother died at 67, full of rage and despair, leaving me good genes, pleasure in reading and writing, guilt, and her guiding creed, "Perfection is the only acceptable criterion." My sister left for Radcliffe when I was 7, and never came back, except for occasional visits. Returning for graduate study, she became the seminar assistant→secretary→companion →caregiver of an eminent German refugee. Her doctoral thesis was accepted, but she never had time for the course work. Childless and unmarried, she devoted her life to the service of others and died at 96 in a New Hampshire nursing home. My brother, in his late 20s, was working on a secret Atomic Energy Commission project when he turned schizophrenic and lost his security clearance. He retired to Vermont to ponder (and publish) possible limitations on Einstein's unified field theory and died of emphysema in his 50s in the Vermont Veterans' Home. He had announced, 20 years before, that he would commit suicide by tobacco.

Ned and I moved to La Vida Llena in 2004 as he developed Alzheimer's. He died in 2013, leaving me his last of many gifts: peace of mind. For more than 60 years, he provided good cheer (and problem-solving) in my life, never complained about my terrible cooking, and never had a vacation that did not include our children. Our children have all led productive lives and cherish his memory, and our remarkably diverse 10 grandchildren are a pleasure to know. I have been very lucky.

Life is a problem to be solved.

Laugh and the world laughs with you ...

Mary Louise Miller

Learning Leadership
by
Mary Louise Miller

My beloved mother-in-law, Mae Miller, was a member of the P.E.O. (Philanthropic Educational Organization) Sisterhood in California. She always said, "If you are ever asked to join, it's a wonderful organization. Don't turn it down."

P.E.O. is an international sisterhood of a quarter million women in the U.S. and Canada that promotes educational opportunities for women through their scholarship and loan programs. One of the six philanthropies is Cottey College. It is a four-year women's college in Nevada, Missouri, that the sisterhood has owned and supported since 1927.

P.E.O. has clearly made a difference in the lives of women all over the world. According to the official website, more than 90,000 women have benefited from the organization's educational grants, loans, awards, special projects and stewardship of Cottey College. To date, P.E.O. has awarded Educational Loan Fund dollars totaling more than $143.6 million, International Peace Scholarships of more than $29 million, Program for Continuing Education grants of more than $43 million, Scholar Awards of more than $16 million, and P.E.O. STAR Scholarships of more than $2.6 million. In addition, 8,500 women have graduated from Cottey College.

I graduated from the University of California, Berkeley, that was within commuting distance of Piedmont in the Bay Area of California where I grew up. I worked for the State of California's Department of Employment for five years while my husband, Alan, returned to U.C. Berkeley for a Ph.D. After moving to Socorro, N.M., in 1967 so my husband could teach at New Mexico Institute of Mining and Technology (New Mexico Tech), I was fortunate to be a stay-at-home mom. There were many volunteer activities in the community in which I participated during the 45 years we lived there.

In 1978 I was asked to join P.E.O. Remembering my mother-in law's advice, I accepted. This sisterhood became an important part of my life. I found the Chapter to be a good way to meet and know women from the community, the various churches, and the faculty wives. I already knew a number of the members and liked and enjoyed their company. After serving in several of the local chapter offices, including president, a group of the sisters asked if I would consider serving as a New Mexico state officer. I would never have considered this for any of the other organizations to which I belonged. However, I knew if I were elected, I would have the love and support of all the sisters statewide.

At that time there were seven officers on the board from chapters around the state. Each officer served a year in the seven positions ending with president. After serving in an office, the sister was asked to move up to the next office. So if one served in each office in turn she would be on the board for seven years. Therefore, the decision to allow my name to be put up for consideration was not made lightly. My children were grown: our daughter, Heidi, had graduated college and was to be married later that summer; and our son, Sheldon, had completed training as an auto technician and had a good position at an Albuquerque auto dealership. My husband, Alan, was still teaching classes and was willing to support me in my decision. I was encouraged by my Socorro sisters' belief that I could manage the jobs on the board capably with grace and understanding.

I allowed my name to be put in nomination for the beginning board office of treasurer at the 1987 state convention in Clovis. There were two other women whose names were put up for consideration. At the convention of about 150 delegates, the three of us were asked to make a presentation. I was asked to give the history of the original New Mexico Chapter "A" which was chartered in Carlsbad, New Mexico, in 1909. After each of us had given our presentation, the balloting began. On the second ballot, I was elected to the New Mexico P.E.O. State Board.

What a turning point in my life! My service on the board turned out to be a wonderful experience. I met and made friends of sisters from all over the state. I traveled around the state by myself to visit chapters, checking their books and meeting routine. I organized programs and training sessions. I handled state business whether money, correspondence, or keeping track of members. Several of the offices such as treasurer, corresponding secretary, and the last two years of service as vice-president and president were pretty much full time jobs. I traveled the four corners of New Mexico from Farmington to Raton, to Hobbs, to Silver City, and all that is between — Gallup, Santa Fe, Roswell, and Truth or Consequences. As you can imagine, many miles were put on my car, and I built many, many friendships. As the years go by I remember the faces but not all the names! I also made close friendships with my fellow board sisters, 12 over the years, with whom I still keep in touch. It doesn't matter if they are in Texas, Clayton or Albuquerque, N.M. Those who served just ahead of me and just after me are especially close because of our experiences together.

As president, I took the New Mexico delegation of 35 members to the International Convention in Atlanta which at that time meant arranging the air transportation and hotel rooms. I was an overseer for the state budget and scholarship committees. A big job as president was organizing the convention over which I presided in Albuquerque in 1994 with over 300 delegates and visitors in attendance. I served for seven years from 1987 to 1994 overseeing the state's 64 chapters. Each office I held helped me learn the duties and responsibilities needed for the next step.

Serving on the New Mexico State P.E.O. Board changed my life since I used my intellect, education, and background experience. I had not had a career in the usual sense, but working in this way for seven years gave me great satisfaction. Another way in which my life was changed is that I am now comfortable speaking to a group whether large or small. Serving was truly a highlight of my life, one I will never forget and for which I am eternally grateful.

It Is Respectable to Be Blind
by
Patricia Munson

Let's get started by getting the most obvious aspect about me straight. I was born blind but have had to live in your "sighted world" so I have had to learn a ton of stuff I understand only abstractly.

My earliest memory of knowing I was "different" from others was when an eye doctor told my parents that they were going to have to let me examine as many things as possible with my hands because I could not see them with my eyes. I never thought to ask my parents how they felt about having a blind child; but since the only blind persons they saw were begging with tin cups outside major department stores in downtown San Francisco, I bet I can guess. I have discussed said topic with many of my blind friends whose families, for the most part, held out little hope for their blind child.

The neighbor kids had things such as coloring books and crayons, so I insisted upon having them also. They showed me that there were lines that defined an outline of a house, a dog and so on. My parents had to raise the lines so I could color within the space. The kids said the crayons were different colors, so I had to label mine so that I did not color the dog orange or green.

I insisted on playing all the games, like jump rope, baseball and kick the can. Skating and bike riding were harder, but I figured out how to do them. The kids were great and helped me find a way to participate fully. Sighted children are never a problem. Sighted adults are the "problem" because they have learned all the negative stereotypes about blindness.

While I had no problems with my pals, I would hear adults whispering about the fact that I could not see and how awfully sad that was. As the years passed, I became very conflicted about my being "different." My family did not seem to want to talk about that subject.

I learned the print letters from my wooden blocks and learned to write them myself and then I learned script writing. Remember, I insisted I had to do what other kids did! Of course, I could not read print books, but I learned Braille. Sighted people had to read print to me. Oh, I learned to type in the first grade and could use an abacus for math.

As I got near graduation from high school, I worried about what I could do after college. I knew of a couple of blind lawyers, but most of the blind people I knew were unemployed.

In college I studied French, English and music but had no idea what I would do with my knowledge. A number of my sighted friends were talking about being teachers so I thought I would be a teacher, too.

However, at that time I had not discussed teaching in a public school with knowledgeable National Federation of the Blind (NFB) members. NFB is the most activist and member-directed organization for blind people in the world, and it was founded in my hometown of Berkeley, California. In the end, I could only become a teacher because members of NFB had demanded that wording specifying that a teacher must have normal vision to be employed in public schools be deleted from the California teacher code.

I had my blindness skills: Braille and that long white cane. I did not like the cane very much because it was so visible and I thought people immediately stereotyped me as blind and "unable." Perhaps somewhere inside I thought of myself that way. I needed a more positive philosophy about blindness. So, for nine months after I completed my student teaching, I took myself to a residential center run with the NFB philosophy that it is respectable to be blind and blind persons can be independent. I learned to be dogged and how to deal with those who would perhaps hire me to teach sighted students. I did lots of practice interviews with staff and students at my training center. They said that I was on the right track, but only time would tell!

When I went to a job interview I would enter the room, shake hands with the employer, find a chair with my cane, sit, and state that I was blind. I would go on saying that I would do the job using Braille and sighted readers whom I would employ and pay for myself and so on. It worked and I was employed for 35 years. In my first assignment, I taught history of music, and I conducted a glee club of 100 seventh-grade girls. I might have been the first blind person to conduct sighted singers. Everyone at that junior high was fantastic toward me. I was free to try anything I liked. My master teachers were "champs" and the rest of the staff could not have been nicer.

I absolutely loved my job! I will forever be proud of the National Federation of the Blind who provided me a philosophy of independence and respectability and the support I needed to achieve it.

First Grade in Three Languages
by
Elizabeth H. Norden

With an American father working in Prague and a Czech mother with only rudimentary English, it was inevitable that as I was learning to speak, it would be Czech. When I was around 4, I am told, my father made attempts to speak to me in English. I strenuously resisted his efforts — "If you want me to know what you are telling me, you better speak to me in Czech." When the time came for me to start first grade, I was enrolled in the neighborhood elementary school. The year was 1940, and much of Europe was already at war. Living in the protected world of a 6-year-old, I was barely aware of world events, although I did realize that things were changing. Like the morning I woke up to find all the windows crisscrossed with tape, or the day I was presented with a gas mask which I instantly loathed both for its feel as well as smell.

By November of that year the U.S. Legation in Prague, where my father had been assigned all these years, was being severely downsized, and he was transferred to the Consulate in Vienna. Once in Vienna, I was again enrolled in first grade — this time in a German school. As is the nature of young children, I picked up

German quite quickly and spoke it so comfortably that soon I refused to speak any Czech. The day that I greeted my parents with an enthusiastic, "Heil Hitler," my father knew it was time to leave. Fortunately, soon thereafter, came the orders from Washington for most U.S diplomatic personnel from around Europe to return to the States.

Frankfurt was the gathering point for this sizable group. We were all housed in a large hotel across the street from the main railroad station. There was a delay in our departure, and a few nights later the air raid sirens sounded. Everyone moved to the basement air raid shelter. Subsequently there was a rumor that the Royal Air Force had been heading for Frankfurt on a bombing raid, but somehow word had gotten to them that Americans were still there, and they changed their destination. This change of destination was most fortunate for us since railroad stations were a frequent target.

One day at the hotel, I tripped at the top of a long, carpet-lined rather formal staircase down to the lobby, and took the full length of it on my nose. As soon as I hit bottom and caught my breath, my Czech suddenly came back to me as I shrieked, "Maminko! Maminko!

Our designated special train finally left, crossing Germany, traveling through occupied France, across Spain, and into Portugal. My only lasting memory is of a stop in the middle of nowhere in Spain and looking out the window of the high train down on a silent crowd of black-clad women, most of them were holding small children, their free arms stretched up high with cupped hands. The plea was unmistakable. While at the time I did not fully understand the circumstances, that image has stayed with me all these years. We finally arrived in Lisbon and after a few days set sail for New York on an American ship.

My parents and I stayed in New York for about half a year during which time we moved twice. So it was back to first grade for me in two different schools — this time in English. In due course I learned English, of course, although I am told my initial attempts were quite a garble. Since English is not a phonetic language, what the ear hears is not always quite what was said. In addition to English, I was learning many other new things. One day I came out of school with a black classmate in tow and announced to my delighted mother, "This is my friend."

In early 1942 we moved to Washington, D.C., to a pleasant residential neighborhood that had an elementary school down the block. As I had just turned 8 and spoke good, if not totally fluent, English, it was decided that I was finally ready for second grade. This was fortunate since, thanks to abundant and nutritious food, I had shot up since leaving Europe and was tall, even for a second grader. I stayed at the Benjamin Stoddard School until the end of fifth grade and would have happily continued on to junior high and high school. I finally felt I belonged.

By that time I remembered very little Czech and had forgotten German completely. In fact, I had lost interest in any language other than English. Unfortunately, this was going to change. It was 1945 and, with the end of World War II, my father, together with a few others, was transferred back to Prague to help reopen the American Embassy there. So that fall it was back to Prague, back to a Czech school. And once again I did not belong.

Subsequently my father was assigned to Italy and then to Germany. It was not until I entered college in New York, in the fall of 1950, that I lived once more full-time in America. By then, both America and I had changed. For many years thereafter, I continued to feel like the outsider.

The adjustment this time, as an adult, was more challenging and gradual. Perhaps it did not fully happen until 23 years ago when my husband, Stan, and I both retired and relocated from the East coast to New Mexico. The natural beauty of New Mexico with its endless skies and wide-open spaces seemed to speak to my soul. Even more significantly, the tradition of New Mexico, predicated on the principle of three separate but equal cultures, seemed to reflect my own life experience. Finally, I found myself in a place that was a good fit and where I felt I belonged. Finally,

"... it's a gift to land where you want to be ..."

Your Farm Should Be Growing Wine Grapes
by
Mary Moore Plane

In 1950 I was headed toward a career in student personnel administration. I'd been Head Resident at the University of Minnesota's freshman dormitory with eight dorm counselors to supervise and next, at Hamline University in St. Paul, I combined dormitory supervision with student recruiting. After many years living in residence halls, I was ready for a new assignment. That came when I accepted a job at Cornell University's student union, first as Assistant Social Director, then Program Director and finally as Assistant Director of Willard Straight Hall. These job titles meant that I worked with and advised student committees as they planned programs for the campus. I spent 12 years at "the Straight." It was a satisfying and fun job putting me in contact with about 250 students as well as faculty and staff members of the university.

My turning point came when I got married to a chemistry faculty member. After much deliberation on my part about whether I wanted to become an instant stepmother, I took the plunge. One thing led to another as we had two more children in our family. But important as all that was, it was not the biggest change.

153

As the wife of the department chair, then provost, then a college president, much time and substantial supporting skills were required. It was at least a half-time job along with raising four kids. But there was more to come.

Little did I realize when I was a child sitting in the car as Dad and Mother visited with the farmer in charge of property they owned, that one day all that "experience" would qualify me to be the farm manager. In 1964 we bought some lake frontage to moor a sailboat. But it turned out that 200 acres of land went along with it. What to do with the land? Area farmers were raising corn, oats, red beans and alfalfa. That seemed rather mundane. How about birds-foot trefoil or crown vetch? Somewhere along the line our chemistry department friends, who were amateur winemakers, said, "Your lakeside farm should be growing good quality wine grapes." A new window opened.

The exploration of what was needed to properly raise wine grapes took me to soil conservation experts to evaluate the soils and weather experts to monitor temperatures at various locations. I also met with field men for the large wineries to discuss types of grapes and possible contracts to sell production and went to the New York State Agricultural Experiment Station to get advice on sources of root stock and cultivars which made the finest wines.

In 1972 we planted our first grapes. Developing a vineyard would be expensive. So Bob was to keep his job and consult on the vineyard and winery, but the day to day activities were mine to handle. These included: ordering root stock, preparing the ground, acquiring suitable equipment, finding and managing the necessary labor, handling payroll, consulting with representatives of the large winery with which we hoped to have a contract, and conferring about the conversion of our large barn from hay loft to vineyard purposes.

By 1975 we had the first production and a handshake "contract" to sell to Great Western Winery. But by 1976 the handshake was

154

over, and we hustled to sell our production where we could. Home winemakers would account for about 17 tons, but we needed more outlets. We determined that we would have our own winery. This meant tearing out some plantings and substituting others of greater wine quality, applying for a farm winery license, developing our label, modifying the large barn to be our production facility and retail outlet, and creating promotional activities. We started programs, including "Ski the Vineyard"; "Kite Fly Over Cayuga Lake"; "Be a Cayuga Vigneron" (rent and tend your own vines, we will teach you how). We took a sabbatical to California where Bob worked in the lab at Robert Mondavi Winery, and I worked with the farm advisor in the fields. We visited several wineries, talked with many winemakers, and learned the intricacies of wine making. By 1980 we produced our first vintage.

Was all this a far cry from student union work? Maybe, maybe not. Skill in working with people to get the desired result was not too far afield, and the newsletters, publicity materials and visits to our winery were characterized by others as "educational." Business management skills were a new educational experience. Promotion and advertising were challenges I had not faced previously. I forged ahead with imagination and tireless energy.

Probably my biggest accomplishment was the development of the Cayuga Wine Trail, an association of five wineries and supporting businesses (motels, restaurants, etc.). This entity could be advertised and would appeal to potential wine buyers from a large geographic area. No one would travel a few hundred miles to visit just one winery, but if there were five all close together it would be worth the trip. This proved to be the case, and suddenly there were several thousand visitors each summer. It is claimed that the Cayuga Wine Trail was the first wine trail in the United States and 30 some years later, it is still going strong and has more than doubled in size. Each of the Finger Lakes in New York now has a wine trail, and there are many imitators throughout the country.

Obviously, I blossomed under all these new challenges. It was fun. I thoroughly enjoyed solving the day-to-day problems and have given myself a big pat on the back as I review those 20 years of active management of a whole new enterprise. Of course, Bob played an important part in all of this; however, he never retired from academe. We were a good team. Bouncing ideas off each other was exhilarating. Both of us took pleasure in teaching people to enjoy wine and make it part of a good life.

Were we successful? Let's just note that there are now two wineries on our old property, so it took two to succeed Plane's Cayuga Vineyard. Wine tourism in the Finger Lakes is a multi-million dollar boost to the area.

Full Partner in Fact – But Not in Reality
by
Patricia Wagner Reinhart

It cannot have been 56 or so years ago in the mid-1960s since my husband, Vic Wagner Jr., was in desperate need of my presence in the office of our small plumbing, heating and cooling business in Albuquerque, New Mexico. The business was started as a small family business run out of the home by my father-in-law, Victor J. Wagner Sr., around 1930.

My husband was having problems finding the right help. He asked me to come in for a week or so until he could hire a replacement for the person he had just fired. However, it soon became clear to me that he needed more than one person. Guess who that lucky person was going to be? Me, of course — that temporary position became permanent for nearly 20 years.

Granted it was part-time each day, but with four children ranging in age from 9 to 15 or 16, it took some careful, complex managing. They were all in school, going to swimming practice, and one played clarinet in the school band, as well. But transporting the kids and being with them in that way was actually fun and probably one of the most interesting parts of my life.

Guess what! I was maturing — conversation was not just about children, but included other topics, as well — managing home, children, office, etc. I had to make the most of each day. I was on the go almost non-stop from 5:30 or 6:00 a.m. until 10 p.m. Although, I have to admit I did manage to squeeze in late lunches with friends now and then. Also, being the wife of the owner, when I was sick I was allowed time off — but, I like to joke a little and say I was only allowed one day off to be sick.

During this time a young couple with two boys, one of them just the age of our second son who was 3, moved into our neighborhood. Because the two 3-year-olds became best friends, we eventually became close to the parents, Don and Vera Reinhart. Don was a CPA. (You can see where this is going to lead.)

I soon realized that our method of handling the finances of the business was not working, and we would need to upgrade our accounting system. This was a family business, and one of Vic's brothers-in-law had kept the books all these years before Vic entered it. But now Mr. Wagner Sr. had died. Vic was doing the job (running the business and books) working with his mother out of the house.

Fortunately, Don Reinhart was not only a good friend, but an excellent accountant and well thought of around the state. Friction at the business raised its ugly head, and I found myself in the hospital. So I issued an ultimatum: "Hire Don Reinhart as our accountant." He was hired and his first idea was to have the business appraised and buy out Mrs. Wagner. Of course, more friction, but it had to be done. Don and Vic met with Vic's mother and brother-in-law in the attorney's office to take care of the legalities. It was a difficult situation, but in the long run it became a smoother situation.

The first event to happen after Don came on board was that I would supposedly cease to be one of the office "girls," as women were called in that era. But it was that era, and it took a while before I carried more authority.

And his second ruling was that I was to receive a salary. This is where the title of my story, "Full Partner in Fact – But Not in Reality," originates. Yes, I now received a monthly salary, although the partner in reality at that time was slow in coming. We were still in that time frame where women who worked with their husbands worked FOR them — not exactly as equal partners.

Don Reinhart felt it was time for me to be a partner — a full partner sounded good on paper and was legally established, but the reality was much harder to achieve. Interesting.

I was not allowed to have any authority over the men. I only had authority over our office manager. All orders or directions of any kind to the men had to come through my husband. I was supposed to be in charge of the showroom. However, when Vic wanted to do something in the showroom that I didn't think was appropriate, guess what happened? I lost, of course, but during each new event that happened, I learned a little more about how to get my ideas recognized. I was always learning and developing a little more self-confidence.

One day a customer (male, of course) called asking to speak to the owner. I replied, "You are speaking to one of the owners." His reply was, "Please (he even said, "Please"), may I speak to the owner." My response again, "You are speaking to one of the owners. I am Mrs. Wagner. How may I help you?" He was insistent, "I need to speak to your husband." This was in the 1960s, and I was beginning to see the humor in it.

I was definitely in charge of advertising, and absolutely no one interfered. But when I knew something needed to be changed, I learned to manage the situation. In this era I knew that men tended not to listen to their wives, so I made sure the change would be presented without an argument between husband and business partner, aka wife. I went to whichever of our business friends agreed with my change, and he or she would speak to my husband. Problem solved, but no credit given to me. As long as the final change was correct, I was happy. Also, years later, I finally learned to say, "NO," rather emphatically, and it usually worked.

In thinking over this period, I believe we were still on Menaul NE where we had built our first very small shop and where I started to work. Menaul was not paved at that time nor did it have a sewer system. Friends and family thought we were "crazy" for building in the heights, but we pursued our idea and it was a success — so much so that within a few years we were looking to expand. We finally located a parcel on Candelaria just west of Carlisle. It was large enough this time to have room for expansion. Quite an experience! Yes, I had been working in the business for a while and had a hand in placement of counters, showroom and decorating. Surprise! Well, move we did, and there we stayed until retirement. In fact, the building is still in use for someone else.

Also during this period, we incorporated. Thanks to Don Reinhart, now our CPA. Vic was president, of course, and I was always the secretary in the corporation's slate of officers. That was fine, most of the time, since I was receiving a salary and supposedly in charge of the showrooms and the office. As I said earlier, this was quite a learning experience and learn and mature, I did. However, the last year, I decided that I would no longer be secretary — that I would be Vice President and that our oldest son, who was already in the business, could be President. Vic would now be Secretary-Treasurer. That he did not like, of course, but so be it.

Our two sons eventually bought the business. Doug, the oldest of the four children, had been with the business for a few years, but Don, second son, had been busy teaching in the Hobbs, New Mexico, public schools. He also was coaching the swim team. In Hobbs, competitive swimming was not nearly as important as football and therefore very little support was given to the swim team. Although he and his wife, Judy, made many friends in Hobbs, they seemed to be happy to return to Albuquerque even though now Don would have to attend trade school to earn his journeyman plumber license. Don and Doug ran the business successfully for 15 years.

Towards the end of my working experience with my husband,

something happened between us that forced me to take a leave of absence from the job. It was not for the common reason many women distance themselves from their husbands. I stayed away long enough for him to wonder if I was going to return. When I finally returned, the relationship between us eventually relaxed to mostly normal. He tried hard. He was a good husband, father and businessman. He was well respected in the community.

I retired that winter at age 62 after 20 years with the company. As I remember, Vic retired the next summer and naturally went through "withdrawal" from working. Although he adjusted, he missed being in charge, and I missed the business.

Within two years or so he began complaining of pain in his right shoulder. Doctors thought it was a pinched nerve and treated the symptoms. But they returned, and he began to lose the use of his right arm. Next diagnosis showed ALS in his right side. He survived a total of 3½-4 years. We traveled as much as we could but finally had to stop. In 1994 ALS took its toll and Vic passed away.

I did the best I could to adjust to being alone and traveled quite a bit, especially during the holidays. When I was more settled at home, Don and Vera drove to Albuquerque to visit their family. Vera passed away six months to the day after Vic died. Don returned to Arizona after her death and began calling me for help to pass the days. After a few months, I realized he was spending time in Albuquerque visiting his family and incorporating me into the visits. Since I already knew them for years, it was easy. He and I knew each other well as he had helped our business and me so much. Eventually, we fell in love and married in 1997. We had a happy life together until his death in 2006 of Parkinson's and pneumonia.

By being a partner in our family business, I learned how to handle my life in a way that satisfied me. I recognized the accepted culture between men and women and learned to make my way within it.

No Place Else to Go
by
Ruth E. Sadowski

I went to nurse's training because there was no place else to go. My folks were poor. I was born when we lived in the small New Mexico village of Monticello, located 25 miles north of Hot Springs, New Mexico. My parents and older sister and brother had come from Switzerland following my mother's brother who was a missionary priest at a small church, St. Ignacio, in Monticello. I was the first in our family to be born in the United States. I grew up speaking German and "Mexican," as we called the Spanish spoken in our village.

My parents ran a tourist court, Texas Home, in Hot Springs, New Mexico, before it changed its name to Truth or Consequences (T or C) in 1950.[1] A lady from Texas was staying at our tourist court and befriended my mother. She got to know me, too. One day she said to my mother, "Why don't you send that kid to nursing training." The idea that influenced the rest of my life was planted.

---

1 In 1950 Hot Springs, N.M., changed its name to Truth or Consequences, the title of a popular NBC Radio program. Ralph Edwards, the host of the radio quiz show, announced that he would air the program from the town that renamed itself after his show.

I always did well in school. I'd gone to a one-room school in Monticello and high school in Hot Springs. When I graduated my parents and I knew I needed a job. We wanted it to be a substantial job, and that would mean additional training. The nursing suggestion from our friend was the only possibility any of us knew to consider.

So, I went off to Amarillo, Texas, to St. Anthony's Hospital nurse training program. To pay for the three years of nurse training, I borrowed $428 from our Texas lady friend. I entered as an innocent, naïve child from a village in New Mexico. Little did I know that I was about to "grow up" in many, many ways. I was to learn nursing — from bedpans to horrific war injuries, witness the reality of people, and see places I had never imagined.

I did well and graduated third in my nursing class. After receiving my Registered Nurse diploma, I worked in pediatrics at the hospital where I trained and took extended study courses at the University of Texas, Amarillo, for two years.

It was 1943, WWII was raging, and the government was begging for nurses. I wanted to be a part of the war effort and signed up. I was not accepted at first because I didn't weigh enough. After two weeks of effort, I'd gained enough weight to qualify to enter the Army Nurse Corp. I was sent to CBI (China, Burma and India Theater) where I spent two years working in one of the early MASH (Mobile Army Surgical Hospital) units. We provided emergency care for wounded soldiers returning from the "the Hump"[2] and sent those who needed further care to the Army hospital in Calcutta. At the end of the war, they didn't need as many nurses, and I was discharged.

However, I had a skill and profession and went to work for Dr. Service, a much-loved pediatrician in Albuquerque, New Mexico.

2 The name given by Allied pilots to the eastern end of the Himalayan Mountains over which they flew military transport planes between India and China.

This job was my first full-time, paid employment and immediately on my mind was paying back the $428 I'd borrowed to go to nursing school. Pay it back, I did — every penny. Dr. Service recognized my potential and encouraged me to pursue post-graduate training in pediatrics. He recommended the University of Pennsylvania (UPenn) and went so far as to arrange for me to live with his parents while I went to school.

The "only" choice of nursing school had now opened many doors to me — that "innocent, naïve child" had certainly moved into the real world.

It didn't end there. At UPenn I met a Polish dental student, Al Sadowski, who became by husband in 1948. I was an Army wife and mother of an adopted child until he elected not to re-enlist after 12 years of service in the Army Dental Corp. We chose to move our small family back to my roots in New Mexico. When he opened a practice in Carrizozo, New Mexico, Al was the only dentist in the county. Instead of working as a nurse in a hospital, I helped in the dental office. When the kids (now 3 adopted kids) were in school, I took over management of the practice and ran the dental office. Soon we moved and opened an office in Alamogordo, New Mexico, where we practiced for 40 years until my husband retired.

It was the decision to take the only known option — go to nursing school — that opened up a much bigger world for me. Once I saw the world, I was forever moving forward.

From the Old Word to the New World
by
Inge Taylor

In 1939 World War II changed my happy childhood in Germany. My hometown was close to the French border; therefore my mother, sister and I were evacuated to a village in the mountains. We were devastated to leave my father behind. When German troops moved into France, we were able to return home. By 1944 all schools were closed when the German troops had to retreat. Air attacks became more frequent and destroyed most of our town of 250,000 people. We lived and prayed in the bomb shelter of our house. Peace returned in 1945 when our town was occupied by American forces. The war taught me that you might lose all of your belongings, but the things you carry in your head and heart are always yours.

Life was good again. I graduated from high school with honors and received the "Abitur" diploma, the equivalent of two years of college. At the Conservatory of Theatre, I completed my studies to become an actress. I had numerous engagements as an actress and modeling opportunities followed.

My life took a turning point in 1953 when I was at my tennis club and met tall, dark and handsome Lt. Tom Taylor. Days later he asked me for a date. I hesitated because "nice girls" did not date members of foreign military. I finally agreed to a date out of town, and we drove to the famous spa town, Baden-Baden.

Tom was sincere, intelligent and thoughtful. We quickly fell in love, and he proposed to me after only dating for six weeks. My soul searching began: Was my love for him so strong that I could leave my loving family, friends and country? Did Tom have the courage and patience to transplant me? It took me three days to say, "Yes." Tom respectfully asked my father for my hand. My father did not speak English, and Tom spoke very little German. I translated carefully, word for word, and my father gave his permission.

Tom was scheduled to return to the USA soon. We had to hurry to get our marriage license and my visa. Tom received the required permission from the commanding general of the US Army in Europe. I passed a background check and physical. We had a beautiful, large wedding in my church and then left for a honeymoon in Switzerland and Italy.

Tom's orders to return to the USA came soon, and I said a tearful goodbye to my family and friends. It was nine months after our first date when we boarded a troop ship in Bremerhaven, Germany, for a transatlantic crossing to New York City. The eight days at sea were difficult. I had left my old world but was not yet in my new world. The first sight of my new country in 1954 was overwhelming as we passed the Statue of Liberty. It was exciting to explore New York City for five days before we left for the long drive to New Mexico. Tom proudly showed me his beloved country.

We arrived in Tom's hometown, Roswell, N.M., to a warm welcome by his parents, sisters and brothers. Tom's job was in Albuquerque, N.M., and we moved there soon. It was a challenge to learn about the different cultures, customs and how to cook my first turkey. I loved New Mexico's sunshine and mountains, but everything was so brown!

I was homesick, and I wanted to find a way to keep my promise to my parents that I would return for a visit in two years. It was time to find a job. I had my translated and notarized diplomas and certificates with me. I had no banking experience, but a bank hired me. I learned that in the USA you are given a chance to be anything you want to be.

I returned to Germany for a happy visit. Soon, back home, we were blessed with the arrival of a beautiful daughter and then another. My homesickness lessened. We invited my family to visit us because they needed to see our happiness with their own eyes.

Our two daughters were in school when my life took another turn. Using my earlier modeling experience, I was commentating a fashion show at our local club when I was approached to teach at a professional modeling school. I accepted and taught modeling, visual poise, speech and wardrobe. Later Tom encouraged me to form my own fashion coordinating company. I developed a business of providing fashion shows to local clubs, organizations and restaurants. We did ramp fashion shows, stage fashion shows, and table-to-table shows. This business required outreach and development on my part and provided work for my modeling students, programs for the community and business for local stores.

We retired, traveled the world and then moved to Nueva Vista at La Vida Llena in 2012. We gratefully celebrated our 60th wedding anniversary in 2014.

I am blessed to have roots in two countries; I am blessed to have the best of both worlds.

She Was My Anchor
by
Ingrid Tollius

Throughout my childhood, I drifted from one caregiver to another. I was born in 1939 to a Swedish father, Gosta Hansson (who changed his name to Tollius) and an American mother, Elsie Welsh Saltus, an aristocratic socialite from Philadelphia. We lived outside Stockholm. My mother left my father and me when I was 2 years old. She returned to the United States with my 17-year-old sister, who  was a debutante in New York City. My sister's escorts were two Swedish men. Later she married one of them and returned to Sweden. Her husband worked at a very large bank in Stockholm. My mother never returned to Sweden again.

One of my first memories is crawling out of my crib, out of the house, along a gravel road to reach Stina, a work horse, in his stall on the family farm where I lived with my father. I loved Stina! Meanwhile, the household staff searched throughout the house without finding me. Eventually, someone went to the stable and found me unharmed in the stall under this very gentle horse. Even at that young age I found the comfort I needed, not from my family, but from a loyal and gentle horse.

We moved from the farm to near Stockholm, and my father remarried. My stepmother never accepted me and treated me very badly. Before I was 10, I took a voyage and at least one flight to the United States to visit my mother in New York City. I remember wearing a sign around my neck with my name on it during the flight. The stewardesses pampered me and allowed me to serve drinks to the passengers. I traveled alone on the plane. A nanny accompanied me on the ocean voyage. The nanny deserted me to attend the many social activities and parties aboard the ocean liner. I frequented the back stairs, hallways and stages, peeking through curtains to watch the adults. Once again, the staff adopted me. In many ways, my life mirrored Shirley Temple in the movie, "*Poor Little Rich Girl.*"

When I was elementary school age, I moved to the United States and lived with a woman who taught me English and saw that I attended a private school arranged by my mother. My mother lived the "high society" life in New York City. She was never very well and never really able to care for me. She owned a building in New York City that had two adjacent apartments on the same floor. She lived in one. On weekends when I was not in school, I lived in the other apartment by myself. My mother had that apartment "bugged" so that she could listen to all conversations on the phone and in the apartment. Frequently, I got in trouble for cutting the cords to the listening device. I discovered that the "bugs" could not hear voices in a long walk-in closet in the apartment. When friends came over, we gathered there where we could speak freely.

Each day my mother gave me $1.25 for meals. I went to Hamburger Heaven nearby. I placed any unspent money in my piggy bank to support me when I ran away. I discovered that a malted milk, which cost 25 cents at the drug store, filled me up and was cheaper than eating at Hamburger Heaven. Eating more cheaply gave me more money to save. I never ran away, but I was very unhappy. A visiting physician, commenting on my health, said I looked malnourished. He insisted that I must leave my mother's care, or I would die.

That fall my mother arranged for me to move to the Indian View Boarding School, the girls living facility connected to Indian Mountain School, an independent, coeducational boarding and day school in Connecticut. After two years in Connecticut, I transferred to Miss Hewitt's School, a private girls' school founded in 1920 and located at 45 East 75th Street in New York City. Most of the students lived at home, attending as day students. I was one of the few students who lived at the school. Kay Gideon was the housemother of the girls' boarding house at The Hewitt School. She adopted me unofficially.

At this time, my mother was very ill and less able than ever to care for me. I lived with Kay. My relationship with her saved my life. For the first time in my life, I felt loved and supported. Even during vacation periods, I lived with Kay at her personal apartment. Prior to meeting her, I was constantly seeking attention, support and love. Kay showed me that I was loved just for who I was. I lived with Kay until I completed high school and left for college.

I traveled in steerage class on the Italian ocean liner, MS Vulcania, from New York City to the coast of Spain. There I attended the University of Madrid and studied philosophy, letters and languages. After two years, I moved to the University of Geneva where I studied languages and philosophy. I completed two years of study in Geneva then went to London for business courses to learn office skills to increase my chances for employment.

In London I met my husband who studied at the Royal Academy of Dramatic Arts. We married when I was 20. My mother came for the wedding and never left London. I did not enjoy business and with the encouragement of my husband, accepted a job as a high fashion model with a London agency. After five years, the marriage ended because my mother, who did not approve of my marriage, took me to Spain on a long trip and our marriage did not survive the separation.

I left my modeling career and moved to Paris where I studied cosmetology and worked in a variety of jobs. Stendhal, a high-end French cosmetic company, hired me. I traveled all over Europe for them. When they asked me to take the entire continent of Africa as my territory, I quit. I, being thin as a rail, was not healthy enough to work that large territory. I accepted a job with a perfume company in Paris working as a cosmetologist in several stores.

My most stable jobs were my last three. The first was working for Paul Mellon, the philanthropist, in New York City as his executive secretary for six or seven years. After his death, I worked for the Martha Jackson Gallery and the Nicholas Roerich Museum both in New York City. On weekends I cared for a Down syndrome child who lived in a home in Pennsylvania during the week. I traveled with her in her family's limousine on wonderful trips and went abroad with her when she was an adult.

I never intended to leave New York City, but when I was 62 a good friend told me I had one month to get out of the city to a healthier place as I was going to come down with a terrible disease. I totally believed her intuition. I packed up and moved to La Vida Llena in Albuquerque, New Mexico, where I had a friend whom I had visited once. As it turned out two years later, I was diagnosed with a very serious illness from which I should not have survived. However, I am still here. My New York friend's vision saved my life.

Many important people passed through my life, but Kay Gideon's love was the anchor that enabled me to do all these amazing things.

174

I Began Life in the Jungle
by
Margaret (Meg) Wente

The setting of my birth became the primary influence of my life, when my parents chose to be foreign missionaries. Independently they made their decisions while in college and medical school. After marrying and completing their training in 1931, they were accepted for service. The mission board determined the greatest need for a doctor and teacher lay in the Belgian Congo. There, far up a tributary of the Congo River, I made my appearance a year later. I joined an older sister. Another sister and a brother arrived later.

Growing up in the 30s and 40s, my life resembled any American child in some ways — two parents, three siblings, lots of freedom for creative play, tree climbing, bicycles to ride on dirt paths, and chores. Although our brick house had higher ceilings and larger screen windows, the lack of electricity differed little from many a farmhouse in the States at that time. We even had hot and cold running water a decade before my Ohio farmer grandfather did.

The differences from life in the States came to us gradually, but they didn't seem strange to us. It was just the way it was. There were only a handful of Americans on the station. They spoke English.

The rest of the residents spoke Lonkundo or Lomongo – Congolese dialects we children knew sketchily. Our studies came from a correspondence course; the Africans attended the local school, where our mother taught the European curriculum, some classes in Lonkundo and some in French. We knew we were preparing to fit into the schools in the States one day. Dad healed at the hospital a half mile away from the house. We learned about malaria, leprosy, elephantiasis, yaws and sleeping sickness.

Other differences included traveling by canoe and steamboat. We had no car until 1946 after World War II, and then it was the mission truck. Dad visited his dispensaries on his motorcycle. The two single American teachers peddled their bicycles over the rutted roads to reach the village schools. Once, Aunt Hattie broke her arm when a large root in the road threw her off her bicycle. And one missionary lost his life on another station, when a dog darted out in front of his motorcycle. Life had dangers besides diseases.

A weekend fair or celebration during my childhood might be the pageantry of "fishing out" a small lake. Villagers dipped their nets in the muddy water catching fish. Other fish flew through the air trying to evade the nets and were crowded toward the large woven fish traps at the outlet of the lake. This continued in frenzied fashion until all the fish were out of the lake. What excitement when fish landed in our dugout canoe!

Entertainment could be a visiting dance troupe of women from an outlying village painted in bright red and blue wearing many strings of beads and short grass skirts. They danced to the rhythm of a drum in perfect synchrony. More frequent and simpler fun came from the boys playing soccer in the field in front of the dormitory, or the boys and girls dancing in a ring to the drum, again in perfect rhythm.

A child's world extends to the community around his or her home. It gradually expands to include extended family, which for us were the missionaries, whom we called "aunt" and "uncle." Our occasional trips to other stations by mission steamer broadened our "family." And eventually a furlough to the States introduced us to our real relatives. I remember little of the first trip "home" at the age of 3. World War II delayed any more furloughs until I was 11. We traveled to the States then on neutral Portuguese ships.

Entering my first American classroom in Ohio resembled entering an arena. Forty-five pairs of eyes turned to stare at me as my mother introduced me to the combination fourth/fifth-grade teacher. The protocol bewildered me. A little classmate tried to explain that we would leave for recess on the count of three: One — turn to the aisle on our right. Two — stand up. Three — start to walk in line. What a difference from home schooling. One adjusts.

At the end of that year, the war was over, and commercial shipping began again. We left my older sister in Ohio with relatives and took the first scheduled ship through the Mediterranean to Egypt. One of the benefits of living so far from our home country came with traveling through interesting places. Dad always made arrangements to see the sights as we passed through, and Egypt had many. I had reached the age to fully appreciate the treasures I visited.

Up the Nile we went by rail and riverboat seeing the Great Temple of Abu Simbel in its original place on the river. That trip preceded by over 20 years moving the temple at great expense to higher ground away from the man-made lake behind the Aswan Dam. From the Sudan we were driven into Congo, met by a Belgian plantation owner friend and returned in his canopied Army surplus truck to the mission at Mondombe, our beloved home. I knew I would stay for only half the 4-year mission term.

The two years passed quickly. At the age of 15, I felt eager and ready to leave my childhood home and join my older sister. I was ready to join students of my age to finish high school and go to college. And I was well prepared academically.

What hit me immediately back in the States were the differences between the limitations of a primitive culture and the extravagant availability and use of everything from tin to lumber to fabric. Paper illustrates this difference. In Congo every scrap, from wrapping paper to the mailing sleeves of magazines, were carefully smoothed and reused. In fact the school's need for a medium to write on was greatly relieved when a student whittled a soft wooden "slate" in the shape of a paddle and brought to school a leaf from the jungle so rough it acted like sandpaper to erase the lead writing on the slate. In the States, paper was carelessly crumpled and tossed. The recycling movement came years later.

Other adjustments for me came in social customs. What to wear sometimes trips me up even to this day. Language, too, left me in a fog. I knew English, but I often didn't have a clue what my classmates meant or discussed. The problem could be teen slang or references to life I didn't know. The fads seemed juvenile to me. And the humor flew right over my head. I laughed anyway.

In college I searched for friends who shared a world view. They tended to be older students or the few who had grown up abroad. Current events both national and international caught their attention. I learned later that my background put me in a category. I was a "third culture kid" — someone who has grown up in a culture different from their parents. Third Culture Kids belong to neither culture and share characteristics with other Third Culture Kids due to their dual loyalties growing up. This has benefits of learning early, for instance, that people differ and yet are worthy. There are deficits in the uncertain feelings of belonging. On the whole, I appreciate being a Third Culture Kid and feel a kinship for other TCKs. These used to be children of military families, State Department parents or missionaries, but now are considered to include many adopted foreign children and the children of immigrants. It was a son of immigrants with whom I found an affinity and fell in love. We were both TCKs.

I feel extremely blessed by the caliber of "aunts" and "uncles"

178

in my life in the Congo. They comprised an unusual number of compassionate, talented, educated and dedicated people. They had a world view, an optimism and a generosity rare in a single group. Their steadfast efforts day after day and year upon year to help others I only recognized to be unique as I grew older. To this day I find great joy in connecting with Congo friends and my memories of those I knew in Congo.

A Casual V-mail[1]
by
Marion Woodham

The most important turning point in my life occurred when I wrote a V-mail to a soldier whom I had never met. In the fall of 1942, fresh out of college, I was teaching English and Journalism at Grants Pass High School in southern Oregon. After my fellow teacher, Howard, whom I had dated a few times, was drafted into the army, we corresponded regularly. Howard finished his basic training in  Texas and was sent to Africa with the Seventh Medical Supply Depot. On arrival in Casablanca, Howard's friend Ray was diagnosed with mumps and sent to an army hospital for two weeks. As the Seventh Medical Depot left for Tunisia without him, Howard said to his friend, "Don't worry, old buddy, I'll have my girlfriend write to you."

---

1 V-mail, Victory mail, was used for letters to servicemen during World War II. The postal service provided a page on which to write a message, then fold and address. After being censored, letters were microfilmed, sent to destinations, printed, and delivered. The same routine was used for mail from service personnel.

181

Soon thereafter I received this V-mail from Howard: "My sergeant admired your picture and would like to have you write to him." Anything for the boys in the service! So I sent a V-mail to Sgt. Ray Woodham.

After being discharged from the hospital, Ray had to find the way to rejoin his group to avoid being reassigned to another outfit. He hitched a ride in a U.S. Army plane; then he rode African trains, buses, wagons and whatever he could find until he finally reached the Seventh Medical at an army base in Tunis.

I didn't know about this adventure until many years later, but I did receive a V-mail from Ray and answered it, thus starting a correspondence that lasted about three years. I shipped homemade cookies and fudge in sealed cans, and Ray occasionally sent me souvenirs as the medical depot advanced with the Seventh Army through Italy, France and Germany. A little reproduction of the Eiffel Tower is one souvenir that I still have.

In November 1945, when Ray was finally discharged and returned home, his old life in Pensacola, Florida, seemed unappealing; so he decided to see some of the country before settling down. I was teaching in Woodland, California, when I received a telegram asking if it would be all right for him to come to see me. "Of course," I wired back. On Valentine's Day 1946, Ray arrived at the home where I was living with five other teachers. He looked very handsome in his lieutenant's uniform. The biggest surprise for me was hearing his Alabama accent, which hadn't shown up in his letters. We were married in Woodland four months later.

The G.I. Bill enabled Ray to finish his bachelor's degree in business administration at the University of Alabama in Tuscaloosa. Fortunately, since he was a veteran, and I had been hired to teach business letter writing, we were assigned to student housing in a furnished two-bedroom apartment on campus. Our $30-a-month fee, including utilities, shot up to $32 when we bought an electric refrigerator. Since war-time food rationing was still in effect, we ate a lot of Spam and canned corned beef hash. Fresh meat required too many stamps. As a result of our upbringing in very modest circumstances during the Great Depression, Ray and I were used to counting pennies and were able to save money for the next scholastic goal.

As I had always wanted to see the world, moving to Alabama was exciting for me, as was our next move which was to Minneapolis. Ray earned a master's degree in hospital administration at the University of Minnesota while I worked in the treasurer's office at the university.

In June 1949 we moved to Dallas, Texas, where Ray completed his academic requirements as an administrative resident at Baylor Hospital. Afterward, he stayed as assistant administrator for three years while I worked in the accounting department of Frito Sales Company. Finally, we were able to buy a house for $9,000 and to start our family.

In November 1952 Ray accepted an appointment as administrator of Presbyterian Hospital Center in Albuquerque, New Mexico. Presbyterian was founded in 1908 as the Southwestern Presbyterian Sanitarium, to care for the tuberculosis patients who came in droves to New Mexico seeking "the cure." (Few found a cure until antibiotics became available in the 1940s.) A new building for general patients was ready for use in 1951 but wasn't fully used until Ray arrived and managed the transition.

Being the wife of a hospital administrator had its challenges. Ray was a workaholic who believed that his responsibilities for the hospital were his primary function in life. His first few years at Presbyterian required building more facilities both to care for the growing population of the city and to accommodate the increasing number of doctors who were coming to Albuquerque ready to join a hospital staff. Each construction project required consultation with many groups and action by the hospital's board of directors. Construction and renovation, as well as improved services, continued throughout Ray's years at Presbyterian.

As soon as he came to Presbyterian, Ray became involved with the Association of Western Hospitals, which included 10 western states, all of which we visited. We enjoyed meeting with many hospital people who became valued friends. Fortunately, we had the services of grandmotherly babysitters so that I was able to travel with Ray to some of the meetings.

When Ray was president of the association in 1965, we were staying in the presidential suite on the top floor of an old Seattle hotel. Suddenly we felt the floor shaking and heard an ear-splitting noise. It was a 6.7 magnitude earthquake! While the chandeliers waved back and forth, and the walls seemed to be undulating, we stood in a doorway and stared at each other, expecting to crash at any moment to ground level. Fortunately, the top floor remained in place.

In 1966, Ray accepted an administrative position with the American Hospital Association in Chicago. Here was another opportunity to experience a different culture. Since our children, Jan and Carl, were 14 and 12, we bought a house in a northern suburb with a reputation for excellent schools. We took advantage of Chicago's exciting museums and big-league athletic teams. One morning, however, after Ray had had to shovel the driveway twice so he could drive to work, the president of the board of Presbyterian Hospital called to ask him if he would consider returning. Ray was ready to go. Thus, our stay in the big city lasted only one year, but it enriched our lives and led to friendships that are still important to me.

While living in Chicago, I took oil painting lessons which I continued to enjoy after we returned to Albuquerque. Eventually, I acknowledged my limited skill in creating art and took several art appreciation classes at UNM. These classes later enabled me to understand and enjoy art museums in New York and Washington as well as overseas.

In the 1970s and 1980s, Ray took an active part in two national hospital organizations: the American College of Hospital Executives (ACHE) and the American Hospital Association. Attending their annual meetings took us to many parts of the country and stimulated our interest in overseas travel. Eventually, Ray was honored as the president of the ACHE, which required me to help plan social events — a challenge that was a pleasant learning experience for me.

I also enjoyed volunteering time at Presbyterian. In the 1950s, I edited letters and reports for Ray and other staff members until Presbyterian could afford to hire full-time community relations personnel. And in the 1970s, I spent many months writing *"A History of Presbyterian Hospital,"* which required a good deal of research and organization.

After retiring from Presbyterian, Ray began consulting in the healthcare field. This work required more travel in which I frequently participated. For years I kept a carry-on bag filled with medications, cosmetics, and other travel necessities so that I could hop on a plane with little notice.

Ray's membership in the Rotary Club of Albuquerque led to attendance at two Rotary international conventions — one in Taiwan and one in Singapore. We subsequently visited many wonderful places in Europe, Asia, Africa and Australia. Each of our journeys enabled us to meet interesting people and gain appreciation for other cultures.

Sharing my life with Ray meant that instead of being engrossed with the teaching profession, I became involved with the people who managed healthcare. The end of my working career meant that I had the privilege of being a full-time mother for Jan and Carl and sharing in their activities and education as they grew up.

Ray died in 2009 at age 90. A random V-mail led to 63 wonderful years of marriage to a hard-working, talented and witty gentleman who enriched my life and the lives of many others.

A Teacher Affects Eternity
by
Maurine D. Yandell

"A teacher affects eternity, he can never tell where his influence stops." — Henry Adams (1838-1918), American historian, descendent of two U.S. presidents

Teaching and nursing were about the only professions females could choose in the early 20th century. My dear mother, who had limited formal education herself, said college was my only choice after high school. But idealistically I thought a nurse could help more people. However, within a few weeks after entering nursing training I was a "dropout." I was homesick, and my husband-to-be was still at home waiting to be called into the Air Force. Leaving nursing training was one of the best decisions I ever made. After quickly enrolling in college and beginning classes, I realized that I wanted to be like a hero of mine, one of my high school teachers, Mr. Delbert Garner.

Following college and World War II there were too many wives qualified to teach looking for jobs. We needed to subsidize the GI Bill to help our husbands obtain a degree. It was fortunate that I had a major in business, and I obtained a job as secretary to the Director of Health Services at the University of Oklahoma for three years. When we relocated to my husband's first job, I also was offered a teaching position, and my dream became a reality.

For 33 years, I taught in public schools. I taught various subjects and grade levels, but typing, shorthand, and seniors were my favorites. An important part of a high school teacher's job is sponsoring extra activities, such as National Honor Society, Student Council, 4-H Club, Key Club, Future Teachers of America, newspaper, yearbook, clubs of different subjects and dances. I also supervised sporting events and student trips out of town. There was no remuneration for these extra duties at that time, but a closer relationship with the students was rewarding to me.

After 58 years, I still receive phone calls from a high school student in Oklahoma where I taught for six years. Kenneth wrote in my memory book, "If one could recycle themselves, I'd still choose your class. I doubt if any student ever thought more of their teacher than I do you." Such thoughts make all the planning, checking papers, grading, and night activities worth it. After 32 years, I still receive holiday cards from Kim and Marlene with pictures of their husbands and children. Poignant memories of these students bring tears. To think that in addition to teaching skills, you may be influencing their lives for the better is rewarding in all kinds of ways. Had I not been a teacher, I would not have had these satisfying reminders of the impact of my work.

As senior class sponsor in a small school, one of my activities was planning graduation trips at the close of school. One year we went to Galveston and another to Colorado Springs. The Broadmoor was our first experience on an ice rink. Of course, we did not stay at that hotel. We also planned banquets, performed 3-act plays, printed the school newspaper, and enjoyed roller skating parties.

In Gallup, New Mexico, at McKinley County Schools I was fortunate to experience working with Native American, Hispanic and Anglo cultures. I sponsored overnight trips with Navajo students

188

to Phoenix, Arizona, and Santa Fe, New Mexico. There were band trips to Denver, Colorado, and Tempe, Arizona.

I took 18 National Honor Society students on an exchange program to New York City. There were many local night meetings to study and prepare for this exchange. When the 20 New York students came west, they were as aghast at the wide open spaces on the way to Canyon de Chelly, in Chinle, Arizona, as our students were at the buildings when we walked down Broadway and rode the subway in New York City. We also took the New York students to Santa Fe and the Sandia Mountains; they took us to a play in Manhattan and the beach on Long Island. Of course, we visited each other's classes with question and answer sessions. Students were placed with families who had hosted their child. To my knowledge we were the only students in New Mexico to participate in this national exchange program.

For me, teaching certainly fulfilled and enriched my life. How boring or mundane life could have been without it. Each year in the fall as enrollment time came it was so exciting to see which students would be in my classes. And each year it was a different group of individuals whom I received and tried to help mold their lives into competency.

Our whole family shared teaching. Teaching was woven into every part of my life. My husband was a teacher and a school administrator, and our daughters attended the schools where we worked. Teaching was a common thread for us. We had the same interest, the same work hours, the same activities, and the same holidays. Teaching and learning informed our understanding of each other's experiences. We worked together in all areas (home, church and school) and immensely enjoyed the successes of our maturing family. Our two daughters Carol and Cathy followed the example of their parents, as they are teachers. Raising these two talented women has been our proudest accomplishment. Carol was a music teacher and a counselor with Albuquerque Public Schools for 36 years. Cathy is a French professor at Carleton College in Northfield, Minnesota.

What more could life offer? Mine is so blessed.

ABOUT THE AUTHORS

Dorothy M. Barbo, born in 1932, is a native of Wisconsin. Her career, for over 50 years as a physician in obstetrics and gynecology with a specialty in gynecologic oncology, took her around the world to teach and train. She retired as professor emerita in 1999 from the University of New Mexico Health Sciences Center. In 2012 she moved to La Vida Llena, Nueva Vista apartments.

Lori Castle was born in Oklahoma in 1927 and graduated from a liberal arts college in Tennessee, majoring in math. She fell in love with northern New Mexico when she and her first husband moved to Los Alamos. Beginning in 1978 she worked as a computer programmer at Sandia Lab. A second marriage at age 32 to Jack Castle resulted in a blended family of eight young adults, now extended to 13 grandchildren and seven "great-grands."

Phyllis Davis, born in Duluth, Minnesota in 1921, was two weeks old when her mother died. Three foster homes later, she graduated from a private girls' school in upper New York in 1939. Having been discouraged from going to college, she went to Katherine Gibbs Secretary School in New York and upon graduating worked as a secretary, and then took a bold step — leading to her story. Her husband died in 1984, and in 1995 she moved into La Vida Llena.

Sue DuBroff was born on December 23, 1924, in Cincinnati, Ohio, to Ruth and Frederick Stern. She graduated from Wells College in Aurora, N.Y. in 1946 with a B.A. She married Warren Du-Broff that same year and they had two sons. Warren died in 2014 after 67 years of marriage.

Pat Esterly is an Albuquerque native, born in 1939, who loves to travel but is temporarily tethered by rheumatoid and osteo arthritis. A hopeless volunteer, she most recently served the New Mexico Genealogical Society as editor of the New Mexico Genealogist, as original webmaster of the NMGS website, and on other large projects. She and her husband Bob have lived at La Vida Llena for over 2½ years and love it.

Janice T. Firkins, born in 1931 in Iowa, was raised in Albuquerque, N.M., and graduated from UNM with a degree in Music Education. She taught in public schools for 17 years and was property manager with her husband in their real estate firm. A widow, she is a new resident at La Vida Llena. She has one son and two Exceptional, Above-Average Grandchildren.

Cecil B. Fish was born in Lebanon, Kentucky, in 1920. She graduated from Mary Baldwin College in Virginia, had a short career with IBM, and married Charles Fish in 1948. They lived in Costa Rica, Ohio, and Albuquerque, N.M., with three children. She moved to La Vida Llena in 2010.

Miriam G. Friedman was born in Brooklyn, New York, in 1934. She attended Antioch College. Following marriage in 1953, she continued at The Chicago Teachers College and University of Denver. After moving to Albuquerque in 1958, she received a master's in Anthropology at UNM. Now retired from a successful career as a realtor, she swims daily and plays tennis several days a week.

Kay Grant is an award-winning travel and history writer who enjoys searching for answers. She has a B.A. in English, all course work for a master's in Broadcast Communications, and a certificate in technical communication. She has been a meeting planner (including organizing a dinner for 700+ where President Gerald Ford spoke), a tour organizer/owner (her scrapbooks overflow with pieces from around the world about the unusual tours she created), and has a mind bursting with ideas of all sorts. Her life is never dull.

Jean Gregg, after living 45 years in Hawaii, moved to Albuquerque where she now resides, continues with "art" and related activities. She has been married twice, has two children, two grandchildren and two great-grands with #3 due March 2015. She celebrated her 90th birthday April 28, 2014, and lives "independently" at La Vida Llena.

Janet Hansche, age 83, was born and raised in Madison, Wis. She has a B.A. in Education and two degrees in Psychology, M.A. and Ph.D. She lived and worked in New Orleans for over 50 years. She retired as the director of Tulane University's Student Counseling Center.

Illene M. Harrison, born in 1933, was raised on a farm near Huron, South Dakota. She attended a one-room school through the 8th grade, graduated Huron High School in 1950, and immediately entered Huron College (now Huron University) while working part-time. In February 1951, she took a job with a new Rural Electrification Administration (REA) cooperative. By mid-1952 she married, continued working, and moved to White River, South Dakota. The rest is history in her story.

Donna Roehling Hill, born in 1932, left Denver after receiving her B.A. from that University. In Chicago and Northshore communities, she produced advertising and employee newsletters for large corporations and marketing services for small businesses and an upscale shopping center. Donna was Executive Director of a Chamber of Commerce for 12 years. She was elected to three 4-year terms as township clerk.

Marilyn W. Hill was born in southern Arkansas in 1927. She earned a B.S. in education from the University of Central Arkansas and enjoyed a 27-year career as an elementary school teacher. She moved to New Mexico in 1966 and to La Vida Llena in 2008.

Charleyrene Hines was born in 1922 in Portales, N.M., and attended Eastern New Mexico University in Portales. She completed her degree and went on to teach high school in Morton, Texas. She later taught typing at Texico High School in Texico, New Mexico.

Louise Hodell holds a B.S. in Education from Columbia University and an M.S. in Education. She taught all levels of students from pre-school to college in three major cities: New York City; Perth, Australia; and Mexico City over a period of 45-50 years. Nearing 90 years of life she currently enjoys living in a large community of seniors in Albuquerque, New Mexico.

Marian Hoge was born (1924) and raised in Massachusetts. Marriage, family and WWII brought her to New Mexico. Education includes a M.A. from the University of New Mexico in Guidance and Counseling.

Shirley Houston was born in 1935 in Pampa, Texas, in the midst of the Dust Bowl era. She finished high school in the refinery town of Phillips, Texas, graduated from Oklahoma A&M University, married Jack Houston in 1956, and moved to Albuquerque. Most of her professional life was spent as a librarian, but in 1985 she realized a longtime dream and opened a children's bookstore, The Story Shop.

Marcia E. Hunsberger was a native of the Indianapolis area born in 1943. During her marriage for 48 years to Gerald Hunsberger, she had two sons, taught elementary classes in Indiana and at McCurdy School in New Mexico, and served as an editor at Los Alamos National Laboratory. After retiring and moving to La Vida

Llena with her husband, she served as Chair of the Dining Services Advisory Committee and participated in the Gathering of Women.

Alice Y. Jurkens entered life in Rock Falls, Ill., in 1924. She graduated from Presbyterian Hospital School of Nursing in Chicago and become an RN in 1946. While working in her field, life changes took an inverted direction into a fledgling business. Her husband founded Octopus Car Washes and they remained principles in the business for 60 years.

Elsie Kather was born in Santa Fe, New Mexico, in 1947. Her parents and grandparents were all born in the state, as well, making her a "several generations" native. She has two sons and four step-children living in Colorado, Minnesota, California, Oregon, and China. She and her husband, Gary, enjoy their five grandchildren.

Joyce King, born in 1930, spent her early and college years in Minnesota. She completed her B.A. and M.A. in French language and literature and aimed to work in Africa. In 1959 she entered the U.S. Foreign Service as a secretary. Later having earned credibility partly through her speaking knowledge of French she enjoyed Foreign Service work both as an officer and a consultant. She retired in 1999 and moved with husband, Bayard King, to Albuquerque. After Bayard's death she moved to La Vida Llena in 2009.

Mary M. Kinney was born in 1931 in Madison, Wisconsin, and lived on a farm in that area for many years. She called Colorado, Minnesota, and New Mexico home for the last 30 years. She has one son and three daughters. For many years she worked as a receptionist/secretary in the medical field and in her parish church office. She moved to La Vida Llena in February 2013.

Lorraine Mae Kunsman was born to Hubert and Lena Ballengee on June 15, 1925, in Trinidad, Colorado. After high school graduation, her first job was as a Harvey Girl waitress, then hired by the ATSF train company. Lorraine married, divorced, cared for an ailing son, and had a full career with the railroad.

Jane Lovato was born March 17, 1919, in Belfast, Ireland. She lived in Indianapolis and Chicago before moving to Albuquerque in 1950. She retired from Lovelace Medical Center in 1981, married Henry Lovato, and they "snowbirded" between Tucson, Arizona, and Albuquerque, New Mexico.

Ann Lewis Lovekin was born in 1931 in Virginia and was reared there and in Maryland. She graduated from the University of Maryland with a B.A. degree. As an Air Force wife, she traveled extensively. In 1977 she married The Rev. Adams Lovekin, Ph.D., making a blended family of eight children. They moved to La Vida Llena in 2007.

Martha K. Mann was born October 1, 1941, in Providence, R.I. She grew up there, graduated from college and then studied at Michigan State University. Martha and Phil Mann were married in 1965. Martha worked at two major hospitals in Boston and moved to Albuquerque when she and Phil retired. People ask, "Why Albuquerque?" They tell them, "Our spirits are happy here."

Marina de Vos Mauney, was born in 1944, in Alphen aan de Rijn, Netherlands. She completed high school at Kranenburg Institute, Dordrecht, the Netherlands; finishing school in Zwijndrecht, the Netherlands; and college in Paris, France. After immigrating to the United States, she used her engineering education as a service technician for Sears Roebuck and moved up to become a nation-wide Technical Instructor in their Technical Training Institute. Later, working for Maytag, she moved to Albuquerque, N.M. In retirement she enjoys snow shoeing, hiking, painting, and friends. She remarried in 2014.

Peg Merrell was born in 1927 and raised in Cook County, Ill. She graduated from Smith College in 1948, married Edward (Ned) Merrell, and lived in St. Louis County, Mo., from 1949 to 1985, raising five daughters and doing the "usual" suburban things. Moving to Albuquerque in 1985, she worked at UNM for 14 years before retirement.

Mary Louise Miller, born in Berkeley, California, in 1936, earned a B.A. degree from the University of California, Berkeley. She worked for the California Department of Employment for five years. She and husband, Alan, moved to Socorro, N.M., in 1967 where he taught at NM Tech, and they raised their daughter and son. Mary Louise enjoys quilting, reading, traveling and spending time with their children, grandchildren, and great-grandchildren. They moved to LVL in 2012 after 45 years in Socorro.

Pat Munson lived in California until 2011 when her husband and she moved to La Vita Llena in New Mexico. She was born blind and partially deaf from the use of forceps at her birth. When she was born (1939), one year before the founding of the National Federation of the Blind (NFB), her family knew nothing positive about blindness. But Pat always had tenacity with the backing of NFB. She was a public school teacher for 35 years in Berkeley, California.

Elizabeth H. Norden was born 1934 as an American citizen in Czechoslovakia. She graduated Barnard College in 1955 and worked briefly in publishing. After children, she switched to Early Childhood Education, first as a teacher, later as director of a children's center. In retirement she moved with her husband to New Mexico in 1994, and in 2012 to La Vita Llena as a second generation resident.

Mary Moore Plane was born in 1927 in Charleston, Illinois. She graduated Eastern Illinois Teachers' College High School (1944); Cottey College (A.A., 1946); University of Illinois (B.S., 1947); Syracuse University (M.S., 1949). She worked in dormitory counseling in Minnesota; then 12 years advising student committees at Cornell's student union. In 1963 she married Cornell faculty member, Bob Plane, and thus changed careers.

Patricia Wagner Reinhart was born in 1924 and lived in Sioux City, Iowa. She graduated from Colorado State University with a degree in music education. Her career was raising four children before entering Wagner Mechanical Systems, Inc. where she stayed for 20 years. She moved to LVL in 2011.

Ruth E. Sadowski was born in Monticello, New Mexico, in 1921 and lived there until 8th grade. She attended high school in Truth or Consequences, N.M., and nursing school in Amarillo, Texas. After serving as a 1st Lieutenant in a MASH Unit in WWII, she married a dentist, became an Army wife and mother, and later helped manage the dental practice.

Inge Taylor was born in Germany in 1928 and graduated with a degree in theater. In 1954, she married Lt. Tom Taylor, moved to the USA, had two daughters, and continued her career in fashion and modeling. They moved to LVL in 2012 where both serve on several committees.

Ingrid Tollius was born in 1939 in Sweden. When in elementary school, she moved to the USA to live with her mother and attended private girls' schools through high school. She went to Europe for university education and had a career in modeling and cosmetology in Europe. She later returned to the USA to work in New York City and, at 62, she retired and moved to New Mexico.

Margaret (Meg) Wente was born in 1933 on a mission station in central Africa where her father healed and her mother taught. After finishing high school and college in the States, she taught for 10 years. Marriage brought her to New Mexico. After her two children grew up, she published her family memoir, And We Ate the Leopard. She moved to La Vida Llena in 2013.

Marion Woodham, born in Portland, Oregon, in 1919, received her B.A. degree from Willamette University in Salem, Oregon, in 1942. She taught high school English and journalism in

Oregon and California and business letter writing at the University of Alabama. She has enjoyed traveling throughout the USA and on five other continents and creating slide shows from her photos.

Maurine D. Yandell, an Oklahoma native, was born in 1921. A high school classmate she had dated since 9th grade became her husband and soul mate for 55 years until his death. Their proudest accomplishment was raising two talented daughters, Carol and Cathy. Maurine received a B.S. from Eastern Oklahoma State College and a M.A. from UNM, Albuquerque. After being widowed she moved to La Vida Llena. When Fred Guyer, a family friend for a decade, came to LVL, they decided companionship was better than being single and they married.

ABOUT THE EDITORS

Susan A. Cho, born in 1943, is a native southern Californian. She earned a B.A. from University of California, Berkeley (1966), and an M.S.W. from Arizona State University (1970). Her 40-year career as a professional social worker in mental health, health care, and Family Practice medical education in Kansas and Arizona, and her own aging gives her a special perspective on growing old-er that has aided in developing the vision of this book. Lured by the special light and landscape of New Mexico, she retired and moved to La Vida Llena (LVL), a retirement community in Albuquerque, in 2005. In 2013 she fully retired from professional social work at age 70.

Shirley L. Patterson, a native West Texan, born in 1933, provided the groundwork for this book. She earned a B.A. in sociology from North Texas State University, Denton, an M.S.W. from University of Kansas, Lawrence, and a Ph.D. in social work from the University of Wisconsin, Madison. For 33 years she taught Ger-

ontology, Life-Span Development, Social Work Practice, and Death and Dying in graduate schools of social work at the University of Kansas and Arizona State University. Dr. Patterson conducted seminal research in "Natural Helping" with Hispanics, Native American and Caucasians and published extensively in these areas. Prior to her teaching career, she worked in the Topeka, Kansas, inner city with families displaced through urban renewal and directed Crosslines Family Counseling Center, a War on Poverty Program in Kansas City, Kansas. She took up photography in retirement and, despite dimming vision due to macular degeneration, has taken and edited all the photos in this book.

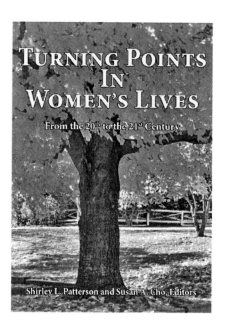

Turning Points in Women's Lives, From the 20th to the 21st Century is the predecessor to this book. Copies of the first book, as well as *Volume Two*, are obtainable from the editors at c.mia@comcast.net or 505-291-5816.

The editors are available to present workshops and consultation to communities who are interested in doing a "Turning Points" project. Contact the editors as noted above.